8 95

Literary Levees of New Orleans

Also in this series:

Literary Byways of Boston and Cambridge
Literary Cafés of Paris
Literary Circles of Washington
Literary Hills of San Francisco
Literary Neighborhoods of New York
Literary Villages of London
Literary Sands of Key West

LITERARY
LEVEES
OF
NEW ORLEANS

by Alan Brown

Illustrations by Joseph Arrigo
and Jeff Slaton

STARRHILL PRESS
Montgomery, Alabama

Starrhill Press
P.O. Box 551
Montgomery, Alabama 36101

Design by Drew Cotten

ISBN 0-913515-44-2

Printed in the United States of America

8 7 6 5 4 3 2 1

Contents

Introduction 6

The Garden District 9

The French Quarter 22

The Lower Quarter 25

The Upper Quarter 33

The Riverfront 55

The Central Business District 67

Further Reading 75

Index 77

Introduction

New Orleans is not just another colorful American city. No, the Crescent City is a world unto itself, populated by larger-than-life characters—both the quick and the dead—and with an architectural style unlike anywhere else in the United States. There are neighborhoods in New Orleans where one can walk a block or two down the street and be transported to what seems a different time and a different country.

Geography partly accounts for the city's unique charms. Entwined with the Mississippi River and bounded on the north by Lake Pontchartrain, New Orleans has swayed to its own distinctive rhythms since its inception as a French colony in 1717. Immigrants who crowded the port city's busy docks joined with the constant flow of transients arriving by steamboat, flatboat, raft, and canoe on the Mississippi to create not a melting pot, but a great jumble of languages, cultures, and lifestyles unequaled in the United States. New Orleans is an American city, and yet it is something else, too, well deserving of its worldwide reputation as a place of excitement, mystery, and perhaps even magic.

Every New Orleans resident has a story to tell, and so do its visitors. The declaration, "I've just come back from New Orleans," just naturally invites the response, "You did? What did you do there? What kind of people did you see? What kind of trouble did you get into?"

Undoubtedly, writers have been lured to New Orleans by the city's ever-changing mix of nationalities and the history that is reflected in its architecture, its food, its accents, and its music. But the city's pace is also an irresistible attraction for the creative-minded. Without feeling the least conspicuous, one can linger in the sidewalk cafes or sit on the benches along Jackson Square and do nothing but observe the human drama unfolding on the sidewalks, in the streets, and in the bars.

Time travels so slowly in New Orleans that in some parts of the city it seems to have stopped completely. Street and building names still proclaim the city's French and Spanish origins. Even the dead make their presence known—names like Louis Armstrong, Marie Leveau, Andrew Jackson, and Jean Lafitte are so woven into the city's culture and commerce that their personalities still resonate. The same is true of the writers who have become identified with New Orleans. Walking through the narrow streets and courtyards of the French Quarter, one would scarcely be surprised to meet William Faulkner or Walt Whitman or Tennessee Williams. They have become part of the essence of New Orleans and have added to its lore through the stories they wrote there and the experiences they had there.

Some visitors complain that—Faulkner's apartment being one exception—few of the locations linked to famous writers are marked by memorial plaques. Maybe this is true, but a marker attached to a building where a writer lived or worked is not really necessary. One need only read the works of these writers to know that they have been in New Orleans and, often, to figure out where they ate, drank, slept, bought groceries, caroused, made love, and, of course, wrote.

So why do people—writers included—still come to New Orleans? That question is asked a lot and a frequent response is that New Orleans is a place where people can be free. One can cut loose during the madness of Mardi Gras or while walking down Bourbon Street, with little fear of criticism. Yes, people do things in New Orleans that they would not dream of doing back in Wisconsin or Missouri. But it's not because the city exerts a corrupting influence on its visitors. It is because people in New Orleans live unabashedly, and it's impossible to stay there even for a short visit without absorbing some of its *joie de vivre*.

A note about how best to visit all the sites in this book might be helpful. To varying degrees, each section of New Orleans can be traveled by foot without much trouble, and so each section of this book constitutes what might be one walking tour. The tight layout of the French Quarter and Riverfront especially lends itself to walking tours. The Central Business District is divided into larger blocks and sometimes requires a bit more street savvy to negotiate; however, streetcar service is available throughout much of the district. The Garden District itself can be walked with little difficulty, but this book's section on the Garden District includes some sites that are well west of the district's boundaries, and these are best accessed via the St. Charles Avenue Streetcar. Happy exploring.

New Orleans

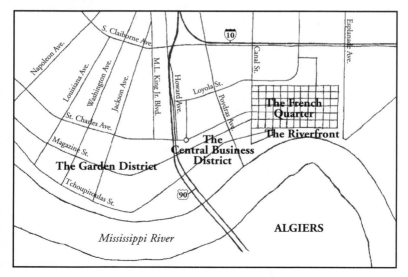

The Garden District

In the early years of the nineteenth century, New Orleans was one of the wealthiest cities in the United States. Barons who had made their fortunes in cotton, timber, and sugar built elegant Greek Revival show-places in what came to be known as the Garden District. Mark Twain described these homes in *Life on the Mississippi:* "Those [homes] in the wealthy quarter are spacious; painted snowy white, usually, and generally have wide verandahs, or double-verandahs, supported by ornamental columns. . . . No houses could well be in better harmony with their surroundings, or more pleasing to the eye." This posh residential section derives its name from the beautiful gardens that flourish in the fertile layer of silt deposited by an earlier break in the levee protecting the low-lying city from the Mississippi River. The district lies between Magazine Street and Jackson, Louisiana, and St. Charles avenues. Its main thor-oughfare is Prytania Street.

One of New Orleans's most visited literary sites is Brevard House at 1239 First Street. This beautiful mansion was bought and restored by novelist **Anne Rice** (1941–), who used the house as the setting in her novel *The Witching Hour*. The third-floor room that served as the slave quarters was used by Julian Mayfair in the *Mayfair Witches* books.

The raised cottage at 1313 Eighth Street was the home of **George Washington Cable** (1844–1925), one of the first writers to delve into the fascinating world of the Creoles and the first native New Orleans novelist to win a national reputation. His short stories and novels were so popular in the nineteenth century that he is credited by some as being the father of the local color movement in this country. While living in New Orleans, Cable supported his large family and his writing by working as a clerk in a cotton factory. Although Cable certainly "fit in" with New

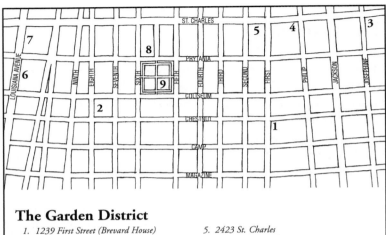

The Garden District

1. *1239 First Street (Brevard House)*
2. *1313 Eighth Street*
3. *2031/2040 St. Charles (Pontchartrain Hotel/Restaurant de la Tour Eiffel)*
4. *2301 St. Charles Avenue*
5. *2423 St. Charles*
6. *1413 Louisiana Avenue*
7. *1525 Louisiana Avenue*
8. *2900 Prytania Street*
9. *Lafayette Cemetery No. 1*

Orleans society because he was a native, he was also an outsider in his own city because many of his ideas regarding race were considered far too progressive. His first and best book, *The Grandissimes,* was written in this house and is considered by many to be the first "modern" Southern novel due to its unflinching look at the horrors of slavery and racism. With the publication of "The Negro Question in the United States" in 1888, he was both hailed and despised as an advocate for the rights of black Americans during and after Reconstruction. Although the popularity of his works has declined, the influence of this early advocate of civil rights lives on in the three houses that are named after characters in his stories and novels: 'Sieur George's House at 640 Royal Street, Madame John's Legacy at 632 Dumaine Street, and 'Tite Poulette's Dwelling at 710

Dumaine Street. While he lived in New Orleans, his house became a gathering place for many notable writers of the nineteenth century, including **Lafcadio Hearn** and **Charles Dudley Warner. Oscar Wilde** (1854–1900) was also a welcome guest in Cable's home, despite the fact that his lecture at the Grand Opera House in June 1882 elicited the same unfavorable press in New Orleans as it had in other cities. Wilde wrote Cable from Galveston expressing a desire to visit him to talk about Cable's books and to see a voodoo dance. When Wilde appeared a few weeks later at Cable's Eighth Street home, Cable's children were impressed with Wilde's long hair, velvet coat, and knee breeches. A neighbor, not as impressed, told Cable afterwards that Wilde was a "fool."

Cable's best literary friend was **Mark Twain** (1835–1910), who had traveled to New Orleans in 1882 to find material for the forthcoming *Life on the Mississippi,* in which his visit is featured in chapters 41 to 50. Cable, referred to in *Life on the Mississippi* as "the South's finest literary genius," served as Twain's guide through the French Quarter. In April 1882 Twain met with Cable and **Joel Chandler Harris** (1848–1908) in Cable's study. In *Life on the Mississippi,* Twain described Harris as being "undersized, red-haired, and somewhat freckled" and also a "fine genius."

He reported that the shy Harris was reluctant to read aloud any of the Uncle Remus stories for Cable's children, who had difficulty believing that this genteel white man was Uncle Remus anyway. So Twain and Cable read from their own work and also read Harris's story, "Brer Rabbit and the Tar Baby."

Actually, this was not Twain's first time in New Orleans. He was a frequent visitor to the city between 1857 and 1861, when he was training and working as a riverboat pilot. He had come in the hope that he could catch a ship to South America. When his plans fell through, he talked Horace Bixby into accepting him as an apprentice. As a young man, Twain liked New Orleans because, he said, "In New Orleans I always had a job." When he was between jobs and hard up for cash, he found that he could earn extra money watching freight on the New Orleans levee, earning from two-and-a-half to three dollars each night. He said that with five or six dollars in his pocket for two nights' work, he felt like a millionaire. He was in New Orleans aboard the steamboat *Alonzo Child* when Louisiana seceded from the union on January 26, 1861.

Twain had mixed feelings about New Orleans, which emerge in his satirical observations in *Life on the Mississippi*. However, he evidently liked the city well enough to take his mother there in 1859 and treat her to a ten-dollar dinner at a French restaurant. New Orleans does not serve as a setting for any of Twain's novels, but the name of the city appears fifteen times in *Huckleberry Finn*. New Orleans is also noteworthy as the place where Samuel Clemens acquired his pen name.

After Cable moved East, largely because of the hostility that his works had generated among the citizenry of New Orleans, his cottage was rented by **Joaquin Miller** (1837–1913) for six months in 1884 while he covered the Cotton Centennial Exposition for the *New York Daily*. Miller, whose real name was Cincinnatus Miller, adopted his first name from a Mexican bandit. During his stay in New Orleans, Miller appeared on the stage of a small theater with **Julia Ward Howe** (1819–1910), writer of the words of "The Battle Hymn of the Republic," wearing his trademark red scarf, red necktie, long hair, and velvet coat. Interestingly enough, this flamboyant character was hailed in England as the embodiment of the Wild West after the publication of his volume of poems, *Songs of the Sierras,* 1870.

In the 1930s, Cable's house was occupied by New Orleans writer **Flo Field**. She was primarily a tour guide in the French Quarter, but during the 1920s she had written one-act plays, one of which, *A La Creole,* was produced in Philadelphia in 1929. She also contributed articles to the *Double Dealer.* A lively and attractive young woman, she met and caught the attention of William Faulkner at a party in his apartment at 632 St. Peter Street. She found him to be a very shy person who did not enjoy meeting new people. After a while, he invited her to crawl through the attic window and out onto the platform with him, but she declined. She was to appear in William Spratling and Faulkner's book, *Sherwood Anderson & Other Famous Creoles,* but was omitted after she disapproved of Spratling's sketches of her. Field met Faulkner again in New Orleans in 1951 when she was an elderly woman. When she introduced herself, he said only, "I remember you."

The home of Cable's literary nemesis, **Grace King** (1852–1931), is located nearby at 1749 Coliseum Street. King objected strongly to Cable's unflattering portrait of the Creoles, and she became a writer largely in response to the challenge issued by Richard Watson Gilder, "If Cable is so false to you, why do not some of you write better?" Her *Creole Families of New Orleans,* which traces the origins of the most important families of New Orleans to European bloodlines, was written to counter Cable's implication that the Creoles were descended from Native American women, African-American women, and women from French prisons. Works such as *New Orleans: The Place and the People* and *Balcony Stories* draw heavily on Louisiana folk literature. Between 1892 and 1906, King was the literary lioness of New Orleans, reigning as hostess for most of the prominent writers who visited the city. Writers like Frank Stockton, author of the short story "The Lady or the Tiger," J. M. Barrie, author of *Peter Pan,* and Joaquin Miller were all guests in King's home. Another frequent visitor to the King house was her friend and mentor Charles Dudley Warner, best known as Mark Twain's collaborator on *The Gilded Age.* Warner encouraged King to write and helped get her works published. By the 1920s, King was targeted as an aging symbol of the genteel tradition of Southern writing in the volume of pictorial sketches *Sherwood Anderson and Other Famous Creoles,* prepared by William Faulkner and William Spratling. One of the cartoons in the book is a parody of the Wayman Adams portrait of her. When King died in 1932, her eulogy was delivered by her friend Lyle Saxon, who had attended many of her teas and claimed that she had influenced his own work, even though she had also struck him as being too "straightlaced."

The 2000 block of St. Charles Avenue lies in what is known as the Lower Garden District. The unusual glass-and-steel building at 2040 St. Charles is the Restaurant de la Tour Eiffel, whose patrons have included artists like Pablo Picasso and Claude Chagall and movie stars like Charlie Chaplin, Brigitte Bardot, and Maurice Chevalier. The restaurant is owned by the Pontchartrain Hotel at 2031 St. Charles. This impressive eleven-story building was built in 1927 and named after Count Pontchartrain of the court of Louis XVI. Many of hotel's suites are named for celebrities who have stayed in them, such as **Rod Serling**, **Anne Rice**, **Mary Martin**, **Richard Burton**, and **Walt Disney. Walker Percy** and his wife, Mary Bernice, lived at the Pontchartrain in 1947 until they found a house to rent. In 1955, **Tennessee Williams** stayed at the Pontchartrain Hotel for a few weeks so he could be within visiting distance of his friends the Bultmans yet have privacy to "do some serious writing."

On the edge of the Garden District at 2301 St. Charles Avenue is the house where novelist **Anne Rice** spent part of her childhood. Brought up in an atmosphere of Irish Catholicism and mysticism, the young Anne created her own oratory in a small back porch of this house, where she prayed regularly and fervently. The old merchants' houses in her neighborhood, many of which she says are haunted, had a profound effect on her imagination. As a child, Rice was very interested in witches and dressed as one when she went trick-or-treating through the neighborhood on Halloween. Rice was also heavily influenced by her mother, a closet drinker who took long naps in this house in the afternoons. Rice's mother claimed that alcohol was like a craving in her blood which was passed down to her by her father. Rice claims that it was her mother's fondest dream that all of her children would become geniuses.

Rice's family moved a block away to 2423 St. Charles when she was still a girl. From this house, she walked to Redemptorist School in the Irish Channel.

In the 1990s Rice bought and restored the house at 3711 St. Charles. Referred to in her Mayfair books as "the pink house," this is where the fictional Mona Mayfair and the other "Uptown Mayfairs" lived. The 1993–94 New Orleans telephone directory actually listed this address as the residence of Mona Mayfair.

At 1314 Napoleon Avenue, at the intersection of St. Charles and Napoleon, one can see another of Anne Rice's acquisitions. The former orphanage known as St. Elizabeth's Home was purchased by Rice in 1993. This three-building complex, occupying two city blocks, is on the National Register of Historic Places. When Rice was twelve-years-old, she rang the orphanage's doorbell and asked if she could play with one of the children. In *The Witching Hour,* Deidre Mayfair seeks refuge in the orphanage. Rice has said she plans to start a doll museum in the Prytania Street wing of St. Elizabeth's.

Continuing on St. Charles across Napoleon, one finds two of the nation's most famous universities. Loyola University, at 6363 St. Charles, is a Catholic school run by the Society of Jesus. Loyola was the center of **Walker Percy**'s (1916–1990) life for his first three months in New Orleans in 1947. Walker and his wife Bunt received instruction there from Father McCarthy for entry into the Catholic Church. New Orleans impressed Percy with what he called its "vital decay." In 1948, Percy became actively involved in the Regional Inter-Racial Commission of the National Federation of Catholic Colleges. During this period, he began work on his novel *The Charterhouse*. Later, in 1967, Percy taught English at Loyola University.

Nearby, at 6400 St. Charles, is Tulane University. This nonsectarian university began occupying buildings along St. Charles Avenue in 1894. At age sixteen, **John Kennedy Toole** (1937–1969) entered Tulane, evidently the first school to provide any real challenge for him. He then taught for a while at Hunter College in New York, Southwestern Louisiana State University in Lafayette, and at St. Mary's Dominican College in New Orleans. Between 1962 and 1963, while serving in the army at Fort Buchanan in Puerto Rico, he wrote *A Confederacy of Dunces,* a satirical portrait of the New Orleans of the 1960s. Unable to find a publisher over the next three years, Toole finally asphyxiated himself in his old Chevy near Biloxi, Mississippi. His mother, Thelma Toole, took the single copy of the book from publisher to publisher until finally, Walker Percy used his influence to get Louisiana State University Press to publish it in 1980. The book won the Pulitzer Prize for fiction in 1981.

Another illustrious graduate of Tulane University is **Shirley Ann Grau** (1929–), who received a B.A. in English there in 1950. Though Grau was born in New Orleans and many of her stories have a Southern setting, she does not consider herself a Southern writer. Her first collection of short stories, *The Black Prince and Other Stories,* treats the black and white inhabitants of the Mississippi bayous not as stereotypical Southerners, but as human beings. Grau attributes the "color blindness" of her work to the fact that she grew up in a well-integrated world in New Orleans. She also transcends regionalism in her novels, such as *The Hard Blue Sky* (1958) and *The Keepers of the House* (1964), for which she was awarded the Pulitzer Prize.

Biographer and critic **Carl Van Doren** (1885–1950) lectured at Tulane in 1932. Walker Percy heard the critic **Cleanth Brooks** speak here. He also received an honorary degree from Tulane. Percy and **William Styron** (1925–) are among the many writers who have signed books at the well-known and highly respected independent Maple Street Book Store, located only a short walk from the Tulane campus at 7523 Maple Street. **Oliver La Farge** (1901–1963) served as assistant professor in ethnology at Tulane between 1926 and 1928.

Directly across St. Charles from Loyola and Tulane is Audubon Park. Named for naturalist John Audubon, the park covers 400 acres, extending from St. Charles to the Mississippi River. This beautiful setting has provided inspiration and relaxation for countless people. In **Robert Stone**'s (1937?–) novel *A Hall of Mirrors,* Geraldine is symbolized by a colt at Audubon Park. *A Hall of Mirrors* won the William Faulkner Award as the finest first novel by an American writer for 1968 and was produced as the film *WUSA* in 1970. The Spanish moss hanging from the gnarled old trees of Audubon Park stimulated the imagination of Anne Rice when, as a child, she took walks through the park with her mother. Rice's fictional heroine Julien Mayfair took frequent horseback rides through the park. Walker and Bunt Percy enjoyed strolling around the park and visiting the nearby zoo shortly after they were married in New Orleans. Novelist **Thomas Wolfe** (1900–1938), just one year before he died, visited Audubon Park with a young reporter one morning after carousing in the French Quarter the night before. Gazing out at the Mississippi

River, Wolfe said, "That's America, and that's some river." The young reporter responded, "Shucks, you should see it at high water." **Tennessee Williams** took a drive around the park with his grandfather and a friend during a visit to New Orleans in December 1951. Novelist **Ellen Gilchrist** (1935–), acknowledging a susceptibility to fads, claims to have been the first woman to jog around Audubon Park—and one of the first to give up jogging there as well. Gilchrist, winner of the 1984 American Book Award for her short-story collection *Victory Over Japan*, was inspired to become a professional writer while studying creative writing with Eudora Welty at Milsaps College in Jackson, Mississippi. She ignored Welty's warning against writing as a career and moved to New Orleans, where she edited poetry for the *Vieux Carre Courier*. She also went off to the Caicos Islands to write poetry. Gilchrist then gained the attention of the reading public with the 1981 publication of *In the Land of Dreamy Dreams*. This collection of stories spans four decades among the rich in New Orleans, focusing on the problems of adolescent protagonists.

The double house at 1413 Louisiana Avenue, between Prytania and Coliseum streets, was the home from 1876–1879 of feminist author **Kate Chopin** (1851–1904). She and her husband, Oscar, rented this double house from the sugar dealer Edward Bebee. Much of Chopin's life during her New Orleans years (1870–1879) was unrecorded, but it is known that her major preoccupation during this time was her children. Her husband was outraged by the number of black "radical Republicans" who held public office in Louisiana during this period, yet Chopin sympathetically portrayed black women, especially mothers, in stories such as "La Belle Zoraide." Chopin's independent streak also manifested itself in the long, solitary walks she took around New Orleans, smoking Cuban cigarettes and taking notes of what she saw. "Ladies" of this era neither smoked nor wandered alone. Years later, the heroine of her groundbreaking novel *The Awakening* professes to Robert her love of walking, which provides her with "rare little glimpses of life." The notoriety of *The Awakening* made Chopin's name unmentionable in the city's literary salons of the turn of the century. As late as the 1960s, some club women considered Chopin's a scandalous name. But she had the last laugh, and her house was designated an Orleans Parish Landmark in 1987.

The stately three-story mansion at 1525 Louisiana Avenue is the Bultman House, which was built in 1857. A century later, Tennessee Williams modeled the stage setting of his play *Suddenly Last Summer* after the garden room of the Bultman House. When its owner, Williams's longtime friend Muriel Bultman Francis, attended the New York premiere of the play at the York Theatre on January 7, 1958, she was shocked by the reproduction of her garden room on the stage.

The small white house at 2900 Prytania Street was rented by **F. Scott Fitzgerald** (1896–1940) in 1920. He began *This Side of Paradise* here, but he tired of the project after a month and wrote two short stories which he sold to the *Saturday Evening Post*. At this stage in his career, he was frantically trying to earn enough money so that he could marry Zelda Sayre and support her in the style to which they both aspired. Fitzgerald did not like New Orleans. Quoting O. Henry, he agreed that "New Orleans was "a story town," but Fitzgerald felt that it was "too consciously that." His disenchantment with New Orleans could have stemmed from his reluctance to be separated from Zelda for any extended period of time. In fact, he left New Orleans twice in January to visit Zelda in Montgomery.

Fitzgerald's house overlooks Lafayette Cemetery No. 1, which is bordered by Washington Avenue and Coliseum, Prytania, and Sixth streets. This cemetery, which was established in 1833, features the typical white above-ground tombs for which New Orleans is famous. For many years, it was the primary burial ground for the city of New Orleans. Anne

Rice and her cousin Bill Murphy played here as children, chasing each other through the narrow spaces between the tombs. It was at this cemetery that Rice's fictional vampire, Lestat, slept. The fictional Mayfairs are buried in a twelve-vault tomb just off the center aisle. **Walker Percy** also enjoyed walking around this cemetery, whose tombs he referred to as "modest duplexes."

In the Lower Garden District at 1718 Prytania is the boarding house where playwright **Lillian Hellman** (1905–1994) was born on June 20, 1905. At the time of her birth, her father, Max Hellman, was trying to set up a shoe-manufacturing business on Canal Street. The boarding house was run by her father's two unmarried sisters, Hannah and Jenny, who were strict with their boarders but kind to their brother and his family. Lillian spent the first five years of her life in this boarding house, moving to New York in1911 after her father's shoe business failed. However, until she was sixteen, Lillian and her mother spent half of each year with her father's sisters in New Orleans. In *An Unfinished Woman,* Hellman admitted that she loved New Orleans, because, unlike New York, where her parents squabbled about money, she could have fun and adventures. She felt she had more in common with her large, funny aunts than she did with her refined, mousy mother. On Saturday afternoons, she and her Aunt Hannah took trips to the French Quarter, where they would buy "smelly old leather books." Lillian, who described herself as a "prize nuisance child," often skipped school so that, dressed only in her underwear, she could read in a fig-tree hideout she had made in the back yard. One day, after seeing her father escorting one of his girlfriends down the street, she threw herself out of the fig tree and broke her nose, resulting in the crooked profile for which she was famous. As Hellman grew up, she became more and more hostile toward the segregation that kept blacks out of New Orleans theaters and restaurants. She once tried, unsuccessfully, to get a streetcar seat directly behind the driver for herself and her black guardian, Sophronia Mason. Years later, she viewed this act as one of those meaningless gestures often perpetrated by well-meaning liberals. She also developed her lifetime fascination with other people's stories by talking to her aunts' boarders. In 1960, Hellman used 1718 Prytania as the setting for her last original play, *Toys in the Attic,* featuring a boardinghouse which is also run by two middle-aged unmarried sisters, Anna and Carrie Berniers, who dote on their younger brother, Julian.

The French Quarter

Although the French Quarter is only one of many neighborhoods in New Orleans, it represents the entire city in the minds of most tourists. The 96 square blocks of the Quarter, also called the Vieux Carre, make up the original colony of La Nouvelle Orleans, laid out by French engineers in 1721. Traces of the city's multicultural heritage are everywhere, from the architecture to the street signs, most of which are in French, Spanish, and English. Many of the buildings, which date from the early to mid-1800s, have steep gables and dormer windows and bear the Quarter's architectural trademark: wrought-iron galleries and gingerbread trim. Many of the older buildings, like Lafitte's Blacksmith Shop, seem dilapidated and in imminent danger of collapsing. However, the impression of decay that many first-time visitors experience is soon replaced by the convivial atmosphere for which the Quarter is world-famous. For generations, out-of-towners have flocked to the Quarter to absorb the party atmosphere generated by its restaurants, bars, and jazz clubs.

After World War I, the French Quarter became the "poor man's Paris" for American writers who could not afford to travel and live abroad. The Quarter had not yet been "discovered" and was still affordable. The seediness of the old buildings attracted writers like Sherwood Anderson and William Faulkner because spacious dwellings could be rented at very reasonable prices. Writers and artists congregated in the "Greenwich Village of the South" through the 1950s. Some, like Tennessee Williams, were so enamored of the Quarter's shabby charm that they lived there permanently.

The short-story writer and novelist **Sherwood Anderson** (1876–1941) was in many respects the Gertrude Stein of New Orleans, beginning with his arrival there in early 1922. Anderson's apartment in the

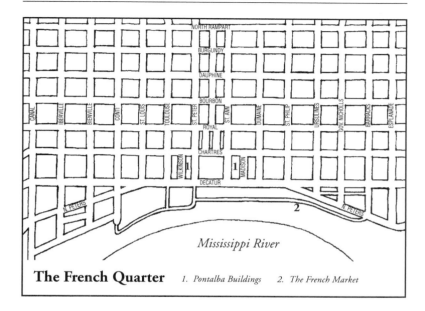

The French Quarter   *1. Pontalba Buildings   2. The French Market*

Pontalba Building on the south side of Jackson Square became the gathering place for young and established writers, many of whom ate dinner on Saturday nights with Sherwood and his wife, Elizabeth. Their guests over the years included **Booth Tarkington** (1869–1946), **W. Somerset Maugham** (1874–1965), **Eugene Field**, and **Edna St. Vincent Millay** (1892–1950), the latter of whom scandalized the ladies of New Orleans in the 1920s by walking around Jackson Square in short, tight skirts and tight sweaters.

In 1937, another famous writer, **Katherine Anne Porter** (1890–1980) moved into the Pontalba Buildings. Her first apartment was an attic room forty feet long with windows on three sides. The $30-a-month attic was, she told her editor, appropriate for a beginning writer. Eventually, a reporter found out that she was living there and wrote a story

The Pontalba

about her in the newspaper. As a result of her sudden celebrity, her landlord found her a nicer apartment in the same building, and she found herself invited to assorted literary gatherings, including a tea for English novelist, playwright, and journalist **J. B. Priestly** (1894–1984).

Walk one block west of Jackson Square on Decatur Street, and you will enter the French Market, one of the highlights of New Orleans. In 1931, after graduating from the University of Illinois with a Bachelor of Science in journalism, **Nelson Algren** arrived at the French Market after riding freight cars from East Texas. While eating a poor-boy sandwich, Algren watched a half-naked black man decapitate turtles and make a pyramid of the squirming, headless shells. Twenty-five years later, he used this scene in his novel *Walk on the Wild Side.* In addition to offering exotic foods like alligator sausages and incomparable muffaleta sandwiches, the French Market also houses a flea market where one can purchase anything from T-shirts to CDs.

Walk north of the French Market on St. Louis Street. At 500 Chartres you can take a break at the Napoleon House, where **Tennessee Williams** liked to relax in the afternoons and drink Ramos gin fizzes. Built in 1814 by New Orleans mayor Nicholas Girod, the Napoleon House derives its name from Girod's plan to house the exiled emperor on the third floor.

At 620 St. Peter Street is the meeting place of Le Petit Salon, a ladies' club organized by the novelist **Grace King** (1852–1932) with herself as president. The club was set up primarily to give the female writers of

New Orleans a forum where they could discuss their ideas. Occasionally, well-known writers such as **Sherwood Anderson** were guest speakers. Le Petit Salon is still an active literary club.

Next door to La Petit Salon is Le Petit Theatre du Vieux Carre, the very first amateur theater in the United States. One of its "amateur" actors was **Sinclair Lewis** (1885–1951), in a 1930s production of *Shadow and Substance*.

In Beauregard Square, also known as Armstrong Park, between St. Ann and St. Peter streets in front of the Municipal Auditorium, is Old Congo Square. In the 18th and 19th centuries, slaves gathered here on Sunday afternoons to dance and chant to the heady beat of tom-toms. Many music scholars point to this location as the birthplace of jazz. **Kate Chopin** listened to stories told by older New Orleanians about the slaves' dances in Congo Square before the Civil War and then wrote about these dances in the short story "La Belle Zoraide."

The Lower Quarter

The Lower Quarter, which is downriver from St. Louis Cathedral, extends to Esplanade Street.

After a period in New York, **Lyle Saxon** returned to New Orleans and the French Quarter. In 1937, using money from the sale of movie rights to *Lafitte the Pirate,* he bought a house at 534 Madison. The 1938 movie version of his book, *The Buccaneer*, was directed by Cecil B. DeMille and starred Fredric March. Saxon had originally intended to retire in this house, but because of the expense of restoration and health problems, he never took up permanent residence here. He did spend occasional evenings in the house, sitting in the courtyard and drinking a Suisse or sazerac cocktail served by his butler, Joe Gilmore. By this time, Saxon was also working for the Federal Writer's Project of the Works Progress Administration, and his duties were taking more and more of his

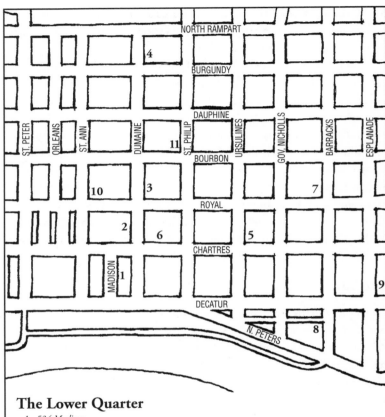

The Lower Quarter

1. *534 Madison*
2. *623 Dumaine Street (Madame John's Legacy)*
3. *710 Dumaine Street ('Tite Poulette's Dwelling)*
4. *1014 Dumaine Street (Pool and Patio Apartments)*
5. *1113 Chartres (The Beauregard-Keyes House/The Le Carpentier House*
6. *921 Chartres Street*
7. *707 Barracks Street*
8. *400 Esplanade Avenue (The Old U.S. Mint)*
9. *510 Esplanade Avenue*
10. *711 Royal Street*
11. *941 Bourbon Street (Lafitte's Blacksmith Shop)*

time. Some of the folk tales he collected for the WPA were included in *Gumbo Ya-Ya,* a book he edited with Edward Dreyer and Robert Tallant. Meanwhile, through the 1930s, Saxon continued to live in his apartment at the St. Louis Hotel. In 1945, he sold the Madison Street house, but not before hosting the wedding of Gwyn and **John Steinbeck** (1902–1968) in its courtyard. Steinbeck described the wedding as a "good and noisy" affair. Saxon got so drunk that his signature in the Steinbecks' guest book was practically illegible.

The raised cottage plantation-type house at 623 Dumaine Street is called Madame John's Legacy. A house built on this lot in 1725 by sea captain Jean Pascal burned in 1788; the present house was built sometime later. Some people argue that this house may be older than the Ursuline Convent because salvaged portions of the original house were incorporated into the newer building. The house got its name from a **George Washington Cable** short story, "'Tite Poulette." In this story, a young man named John wills his parents' house to a quadroon servant named Zalli, who is referred to as "Madame John," even though she is not his wife. Later, she sells her house and deposits the money in a bank which fails. This house also appears briefly in the movie version of *Interview with a Vampire.*

The house at 710 Dumaine is known as 'Tite Poulette's Dwelling. That name, like Madame John's Legacy, is from the same short story. 'Tite Poulette was Zalli's child.

Tennessee Williams's last permanent home in New Orleans was at the Pool and Patio Apartments at 1014 Dumaine Street. He seems to have originally bought the building as an investment, but he liked it so much that he said in his *Memoirs* that he would want to die here. Williams moved his furniture, including the prized brass bed in which he hoped to pass his final moments, into the second floor main apartment in 1972 and from then on stayed at the Dumaine Street building whenever he was in New Orleans. The apartment was decorated with a drawing by Jean Cocteau and a painting of Arthur Rimbaud, his favorite poet. Williams soon became a fixture in the neighborhood, eating and drinking in nearby restaurants and bars or painting on an easel set up by the patio. Williams gave several interviews on the patio, including one to Dick Cavett and another in the rain to a German film crew who huddled under the shelter of a banana tree while he sat out in the open and got drenched. He also walked up Rampart Street for his daily swim at the New Orleans Athletic Club. He did swim sometimes in his own pool, but he preferred the artesian water at the Club. In fact, one of Williams's neighbors recalled seeing him one cold winter morning walk over to his pool, remove his coat, put on his diving cap, and dive in. Williams spent his days in his Dumaine apartment working on his plays and his nights writing his *Memoirs.*

The Greek Revival raised cottage at 1113 Chartres dates to 1826 and is known variously as the Beauregard-Keyes House and as the Le Carpentier House, after its builder, Joseph Le Carpentier. The Keyes part of the name is from novelist **Frances Parkinson Keyes**, who bought the house in the 1940s and lived here until her death in 1970. She converted the slave quarters of the house to a studio where she wrote many books about New Orleans, such as *Dinner at Antoine's* and *Steamboat Gothic.* The house still holds her extensive doll collection and Victorian doll house. The Beauregard part of the house's name is from Confederate general Pierre Gustave Tousant Beauregard, who rented an apartment here for a brief period after the Civil War. He had directed the bombardment of Fort Sumter in 1861.

A sordid episode from the house's past attracted novelist **Rex Beach** (1877–1949) to New Orleans. Corado Giacona, a wealthy Sicilian wine merchant, lived here around the turn of the century. Like many Italian-Americans living in New Orleans at the time, Giacona was pressured by the Mafia to pay protection money. Giacona refused, and one night in 1909, four thugs broke into the house to murder the family. However, Giacona and his sons were expecting them and had armed themselves. In the ensuing gun battle, three Mafiosi toughs were killed and one was critically wounded. Beach, who is best-known for his oft-filmed novel *The Spoilers,* came to New Orleans in 1911 to research Mafia activity. He was particularly interested in the Mafia riots that plagued New Orleans at the turn of the century. The resulting book was entitled *The Net* (1911). A short story, entitled "The Crimson Gardenia" is also set in New Orleans.

In 1950, New Orleans native **Shirley Ann Grau** moved, with a close friend, Mary Rohrberger, into an apartment at 921 Chartres Street. Grau had just graduated from Sophie Newcomb College, Tulane University's women's college, where she studied writing under Dr. **John Husband** and wrote several stories, one of which appeared in *Surf,* a New Orleans literary magazine. While living on Chartres Street, Grau was doing graduate study in Renaissance and metaphysical poetry at Tulane University. This was despite her father's warning that he would not support her in graduate school unless she pursued a career more practical than writing. Although she left Tulane in 1951 without finishing her degree, Grau continued to live and write in the Chartres apartment until her 1955 marriage to Tulane philosophy professor James Kern Feibleman. After Grau published "The Sound of Silver," a rewrite of a story she had written at Sophie Newcomb, and "White Girl, Fine Girl" in 1955 and *The Black Prince and Other Stories* in 1954, her father must have been convinced that his daughter could make a living as a writer.

The low brick building at 707 Barracks Street, just off Royal Street, was **John James Audubon**'s first studio in New Orleans. He rented this building in 1821 and lived there four months before moving to West Feliciana Parish. His *Journal* indicates that by the fall of 1821, he had completed "62 drawings of Birds & Plants, 3 Quadrupeds, 2 Snakes, and 50 Portraits of all sorts." He returned to the Barataria section of New Orleans in 1837 to paint and sketch. Audubon's lasting New Orleans legacy includes Audubon Park, with its centerpiece statue of the painter, and a bust and portrait of him and a first-edition copy of *Birds of America* in the Louisiana State Museum, Natural Science Division.

The Old U.S. Mint at 400 Esplanade, built in 1835 and remodeled in 1861, is remembered primarily for its Civil War history. Confederate coins were minted here after the Mint was seized by Confederate forces; and later, following the city's surrender to Admiral Farragut's fleet, William Mumford was hanged from a gibbet projecting from a peristyle of the mint for having seized the American flag and dragging it through the muddy city streets. However, the Old U.S. Mint is also noteworthy as the site of the only memorial to **Tennessee Williams** in the French Quarter. The "Streetcar Named Desire" display on the grounds of the Mint commemorates the play that has shaped audience's views of New Orleans throughout the world since its publication in 1947.

John Dos Passos (1896–1970) took a seedy little room at 510 Esplanade Avenue in February 1924. The apartment had a blue bed, a raspberry-colored ceiling, and walls that resembled a "peeling apricot." Dos Passos was alone when he first arrived, a situation that was conducive to writing. Before long, he became friends with William McComb, a reporter for the New Orleans *Item.* The two men ate together often; their favorite cafe was called the Original Tripoli. Before he left the city in March, Dos Passos met Sherwood Anderson and probably met William Faulkner. The book that Dos Passos was writing, the highly experimental *Manhattan Transfer,* is viewed by critics as one of his most important works. In this novel, Dos Passos first expressed his disillusionment with America, a theme that was to receive further development in his most famous work, the *U.S.A.* trilogy. In the letters he wrote from New

Orleans, Dos Passos indicated that he enjoyed all that the French Quarter had to offer, especially the French cuisine, although he seems to have left with the impression that the entire population was "reeking with alcohol" and that "horse racing and cap shooting and whoring and bawdry" ran rampant.

Truman Capote (1924–1984) returned to the city of his birth in January 1945 and rented a room at 711 Royal Street to work on his first novel, *Other Voices, Other Rooms.* He came here to work because his habit of working all night and sleeping all day was beginning to worry his Aunt Lucille in Alabama. Despite the street noise generated by tourists during the day and soldiers and sailors at night, Capote was able to finish part of his novel and several short stories as well. Capote's attempt to make a little money by selling his paintings proved unsuccessful, and he then sought fame and fortune in New York. He referred to his short stay in New Orleans as "the freest time of my life. I had no commitments to anyone or anybody." The apartment where Capote lived is now above an antique store.

Lafitte's Blacksmith Shop at 941 Bourbon Street may be the Quarter's most memorable bar. Built in 1772, the structure is reputed to have been the smithy of the pirate Jean Lafitte. Viewed from the outside, the building appears to be in imminent danger of falling down. Its front wall leans inward, and its brick-and-cypress construction is visible where the exterior stucco has fallen off. Writers like **Tennessee Williams** have been attracted to the bar's unique atmosphere for generations.

Various New Orleans locations, though mostly undocumented as to specific addresses, are linked to the renegade poet **Charles Bukowski** (1920–1994). He came to New Orleans in 1942 on a Trailways bus from southern California and within 24 hours had been ordered by a streetcar conductor to move from the back of the car to the front because as a white man it violated the Jim Crow laws of that era for him to sit in the black section. Bukowski found a cheap apartment and began writing fantasy stories to relieve the tedium of his jobs at a magazine distribution office and a small newspaper. Later he drifted away and evidently did not return to New Orleans until 1965. In the intervening years, he had become well-known in literary circles as both a talented poet and an eccentric, often self-destructive, brawling, drinking, carousing personality.

One of Bukowski's earliest champions was Jon Edgar Webb, editor of the New Orleans literary journal, *Outsider,* which had published such avant-garde writers as Gregory Corso, Allen Ginsberg, Lawrence Ferlinghetti, Henry Miller, and William Burroughs. Webb had been one of the first to acknowledge Bukowski's poetic genius, but he was concerned that Bukowski's lifestyle was destroying his ability to write. Webb tracked Bukowski down and offered him the chance to come to New Orleans to work. He arrived on a train, drunk, and moved into an apartment around the corner from the Webbs' workshop-apartment on Royal Street. The building was owned by a gentle lady named Minnie Segate, owner of a small cafe, the Cajun Kitchen. She cooked for him and did his washing and ironing. Bukowski also made friends with a deaf-mute with whom he communicated by writing on paper napkins while drinking in the Bourbon House.

Inspired by the city's genteel seediness, Bukowski began writing ten to fifteen poems a day. Before long, the Webbs' small apartment, including the bathtub, was filled with hand-set leaves of Bukowski's poems, which eventually were bound by the Webbs into Bukowski's first book-length collection, *Crucifix in a Deathhand,* (1965). Bukowski continued to contribute poems in the late 1960s and early 1970s to another New Orleans publication, *NOLA Express,* which publicized anything so long as it was interesting and outrageous. Bukowski's poetry, riddled with sex, violence, and profanity, was certainly that. During his time in New

Orleans, he was a regular visitor to the Ursulines Street offices of the *NOLA Express.*

Bukowski published more than forty volumes of poetry, but remained largely unknown to the public until the release of the movie *Barfly,* for which he wrote the semi-autobiographical screenplay. Mickey Rourke (as the Bukowski character) and Faye Dunaway starred.

The Upper Quarter

The Upper Quarter runs from Canal Street to the St. Louis Cathedral, encompassing the area west of the cathedral. However, the Quarter officially ends at Iberville.

Canal Street made a big impression on **Mark Twain** when he traveled to New Orleans in 1882 to visit **George Washington Cable** and **Joel Chandler Harris**. In *Life on the Mississippi,* Twain said that Canal Street was "finer and more attractive and stirring than formerly, with its drifting crowds of people, its several processions of hurrying street cars, and—toward evening—its broad second-story verandahs crowded with gentlemen and ladies clothed according to the latest mode." However, he also asserted that there was no "architecture" on Canal Street. He cites as an example the U.S. Custom House, which occupies the block bounded by Canal, Decatur, Iberville, and North Peters streets. Twain said that the Customs House's appearance was "inferior to a gasometer" and that it looked like a state prison.

Napoleon House at 500 Chartres is certainly one of the most fabled houses in the Quarter. The house was built in 1814 for Mayor Nicolas Girod, who wanted to rescue Napoleon Bonaparte from the prison in St. Helena and put him up here. Unfortunately, Napoleon died before the mayor's plan could be executed. The house has been a popular bar and restaurant for most of the twentieth century. **Tennessee Williams** (1911–1983) enjoyed drinking here while taking a break from writing.

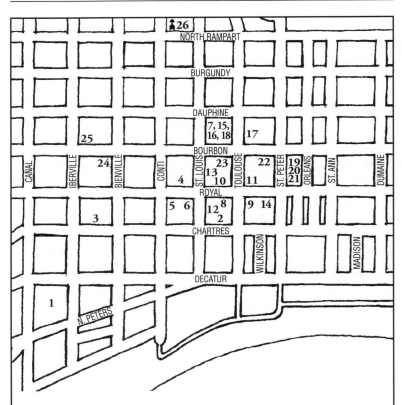

The Upper Quarter

1. U.S. Custom House
2. 500 Chartres
3. 214 Royal
4. 406 Royal
5. 413 Royal
6. 429 Royal
7. 722 Toulouse
8. 536 Royal
9. 612 Royal
10. 537 Royal
11. 613 Royal (The Court of Two Sisters)
12. 621 St. Louis
13. 713 St. Louis (Antoine's)
14. 640 Royal
15. 505 Dauphine
16. 719 Toulouse
17. 722 Toulouse
18. 727 Toulouse (Maison de Ville)
19. 616 St. Peter Street
20. 620 St. Peter
21. 632 St. Peter
22. 623 Bourbon
23. 516 Bourbon
24. 238 Bourbon (The Old Absinthe House)
25. 209 Bourbon
26. 400 Basin (St. Louis Cemetery No. 1)

The Monteleone Hotel at 214 Royal Street is a celebrated New Orleans landmark whose distinctive features include beautiful crystal chandeliers. This is the hotel where **Tennessee Williams** stayed with his 94-year-old grandfather, William Dakin, in December 1951. Williams said that two weeks after checking in, he received a basket of fruit from the proprietor who had just discovered that Williams was a guest. During this time, Williams and his grandfather were photographed and interviewed on radio programs. Somehow, Williams also found time to work on his play *Camino Real*. **Truman Capote** (1924–1984) was almost born in the Monteleone Hotel. His mother had considered aborting her unborn child because she regretting marrying her husband, Arch. However, Arch wanted a son, and rented a suite in the Monteleone while he arranged to have the baby delivered by Dr. E. R. King, one of the city's best obstetrician-gynecologists. The baby was born at the Touro Infirmary on September 30, 1924. Arch named him after an old friend from military school, Truman Moore.

The historic old home at 406 Royal Street was the site of one of New Orleans's most fashionable literary salons in the late nineteenth century. Shortly after moving to New Orleans so that her husband could take the position of editor of the *Daily Picayune,* **Mollie E. Moore Davis** (1844–1909) began bringing together local writers and authors who had national and even international reputations. These gatherings, which Davis called "Fridays," attracted "belles, beaux, papas, mamas, poets, painters, musicians, journalists, statesmen, scientists, churchmen, men and women of letters, foreign and homebred officers, military and naval." Some of her more notable guests were **George Washington Cable**, **Kate Chopin**, and "**Pearl Rivers**," (a.k.a. **Eliza Nicholson**). Nicholson, the owner and editor of the *New Orleans Picayune* and the first woman publisher of a daily newspaper in the United States, published a small book of poems entitled *Lyrics.*

Davis's good friend **Frank Stockton** (1834–1902) was also a frequent guest. A writer of science fiction and children's stories, Stockton's best-known work is his widely anthologized short story "The Lady or the Tiger?" Stockton wrote a love story about New Orleans entitled "The Romance of a Mule-Car" in *Afield or Afloat* (1900). Another frequent guest, **Eugene Field**, took time to scour the antique shops and to visit the old Begue Restaurant whenever he made a trip for one of Davis's parties. Two of the poems that he wrote about New Orleans are "Good Children Street" and "Dr. Sam."

The woman Davis called the "brightest of story tellers," **Ruth McEnery Stuart** (1856–1964), regaled Davis's guests with her stories of plantation Negroes. Even after she moved to New York in 1888, she continued to use Louisiana locales in her stories. Her books with New Orleans settings include a children's novel, *The Story of Babette* (1902), and *Solomon Crow's Christmas Pockets* (1896), a collection of African-American fables.As a rule, Davis's guests gave readings and told ghost stories. Davis herself wrote plays, novels, poems, and short stories, many of which have a New Orleans setting. Davis's works actually outsold Kate Chopin's at the turn of the century. Interestingly, Davis's short story "A Bamboula" reflects the influence of Kate Chopin's "La Belle Zoraide." Although today her work is mainly of historic interest, Davis is remembered as one of New Orleans's most popular hostesses.

The building with the monogrammed balcony that stands at 413 Royal Street was the home of two of the city's earliest writers, **Dominique** and **Adrien Rouquette**. Like most New Orleans writers who worked between 1820 and 1860, the Rouquette brothers wrote in French and were heavily influenced by the French Romantics. They lived in this house with their father, a wealthy New Orleans merchant, until they were old enough to go to college in France. Their first books of poems were published in Paris and were widely praised by writers like Victor Hugo and Sainte-Beuve. After publishing only two books of poems, Dominique returned to New Orleans as its "unofficial" bard. Adrien returned to New Orleans after the 1841 publication of *Les Sevanes* in Paris and became a missionary to the Choctaws living near New Orleans. However, Adrien continued writing up to the end of his life. Like his brother, Adrien's themes revolved around the beauty of Louisiana.

536 Royal Street

Tennessee Williams lived for a brief time at the house at 429 Royal Street. After taking the bus from St. Louis to New Orleans in December 1938, Williams stayed here before moving to the boarding house just around the corner at 722 Toulouse Street. Of his early years in the French Quarter, Williams said, "In New Orleans I felt a freedom. I could catch my breath here."

The houses at 536 Royal Street and 612 Royal Street were the homes of **Lyle Saxon** (1891–1946), known by his literary friends as "Mr. French Quarter." Saxon lived intermittently at these two houses while working as a reporter for the *Times-Picayune*. Although it was rumored that Saxon's "plantation background" provided him with the money to buy and restore old houses, the truth is that he rented or bought his French Quarter houses during a buyer's market. In fact, Saxon liked to brag to his friends that in 1920 he leased the sixteen-room house at 612 Royal Street for sixteen dollars a month. Saxon's first literary salon was conducted at the house on 612 Royal Street and then followed him in his

various moves through the Quarter. Saxon's restoration efforts caught on
with the other residents in the Quarter, and soon it was said that Lyle
Saxon had spearheaded the movement to save the Vieux Carre from ruin.
Some believe, however, that Saxon's real motive was to transport himself
to the romantic 1930s when Royal Street was the most beautiful thor-
oughfare in New Orleans.

By the time he "retired" from the *Times-Picayune* in 1926, he was
possibly the highest paid reporter in New Orleans. As Saxon's work load
began to decline in 1924-1926, he began forming close relationships with
writers who had sought refuge from the "real world" in New Orleans. He
also found the time to write four books during a three-year period at the
end of the 1920s: *Father Mississippi* (1927), *Fabulous New Orleans*
(1928), *Old Louisiana* (1929), and *Lafitte the Pirate* (1930). These books
earned him a reputation as one of Louisiana's foremost regional writers,
though the quality of his books is uneven. His best works are vivid
portrayals of the state's history; his worst are potboilers in which he
adapted grotesque or sensational stories from earlier Louisiana writers,
like George Washington Cable. The myth of Saxon's having grown up on
his uncle's huge plantation probably came from these books.

Saxon's role as host to New Orleans's literati began after illness forced
him to quit his full-time job at the *Times-Picayune*. American author and
anthropologist **Oliver La Farge** (1901–1963), a resident in the Quarter
and a close friend of Saxon's, told him years later that he thought he had
"written himself out" after the publication of *Laughing Boy* in 1929.
William Spratling, another of Saxon's neighbors, depicted him in
Sherwood Anderson and Other Famous Creoles as lying against a pillow and
reading Strachly's *Eminent Victorians*. Saxon befriended **William Faulkner**
soon after the future Nobel winner arrived in New Orleans. The two men
probably met at a party at one of Saxon's houses or at Sherwood
Anderson's apartment. **Hamilton Basso** (1904–1964), who was raised on

the 1200 block of Decatur Street, became a longtime friend of Saxon's and was also a frequent guest of Sherwood Anderson's. He moved to North Carolina to write about New Orleans's early history. Basso also became a good friend of William Faulkner when he took Faulkner for a ride in a two-seater Wright Whirlwind airplane. Basso was doing a feature story on "The Gates Flying Circus," and Faulkner enjoyed "looping-the-loop" over the Mississippi River so much that he took a half-dozen more rides in the plane. Basso's most famous novel is *The View from Pompey's Head,* which deals with prejudice in a small Southern town. The film version, produced in 1954, starred Richard Egan and Dana Wynter. British writer **Lord Dunsany** (1878–1957) stopped by to visit Saxon on while visiting America in the 1920s. Dunsany wrote more than 50 books, but he is best known for his stories of the supernatural. Saxon assisted his longtime friend **Stark Young** (1881–1963), author of the Civil War novel *So Red the Rose,* with collecting background material for a collection of short stories on East Feliciana parish, appropriately entitled *Feliciana.* **T. S. Stribling** (1881–1965), winner of the Pulitzer Prize for *The Store,* came to New Orleans in 1937 to address the staff of the Federal Writers' Project in 1937. Mystery writer **Gwen Bristow** (1903–1980) was a likely Saxon visitor; she had been a reporter for the *Times-Picayune* from 1925–1934. She began writing mystery novels set in New Orleans with her husband, Bruce Manning, but branched out into historical fiction with her trilogy of Louisiana novels. Three of her novels—*The Invisible Host, Tomorrow Is Forever,* and *Jubilee Trail*—were made into films.

Saxon left New Orleans in 1926 for New York, where he played host to other expatriate Southern writers who called themselves the Southern Protective Society. It was rumored that Saxon had to leave New Orleans because of an affair with a married woman, Olive Boullemet.

Saxon's best friend was **Roark Bradford**, a fellow reporter at the *Times-Picayune.* The two men inadvertently contributed to the folklore of the French Quarter in the early 1920s when they made up the character of Annie Christmas one day when they were desperate for a newsworthy story. In the resulting article, they claimed to have found some old accounts of a legendary river lady who had the superhuman powers of other better-known folk heroes such as Mike Fink. Saxon embellished the exploits of Annie Christmas in two of his books. When the Alabama folklorist **Carl Carmer** (1893–1976) asked Saxon and Bradford for folk tales for his book *The Hurricane's Children,* they fed him stories of their bogus heroine. Carmer went on to devote an entire chapter to Annie Christmas.

The Court of Two Lions at 537 Royal was bought by **Vincent Nolte** in 1819 from Jean Francois Merieult. Nolte was an international financier who lived in New Orleans periodically from 1808–1838 and conducted his cotton commission business in this house from 1819 to 1827. Nolte wrote about his adventures in a book entitled *Fifty Years in Both Hemispheres* (1854). Herbie Allen's novel *Anthony Adverse* and the 1936 film *Anthony Adverse,* starring Frederic March and Olivia de Havilland, were based on Nolte's autobiography. Another writer with a connection to the Court of Two Lions is the American novelist **Winston Churchill** (1871–1947). His most famous novel, *The Crisis,* is set during the American Civil War. He became acquainted with the French Quarter when he visited it around the turn of the century and was so fascinated by the Court of Two Lions that he used it in his novel *The Crossing,* which is partly set in New Orleans and deals with the acquisition of the Louisiana Territory from France. In this novel, the Court of Two Lions is the home of his heroine.

Tennessee Williams also enjoyed sitting at the patio bar in the Court of Two Sisters at 613 Royal Street. This restaurant, noted for its beautiful courtyard, is named after two sisters who once ran a variety store at this location. The restaurant is mentioned in Williams's play *Vieux Carre.* In

Anne Rice's novel *The Witching Hour,* Aaron Lightner had lunch with Stella Mayfair here.

The First National Bank of Commerce Building at 621 St. Louis Street now occupies the site of the St. Louis Hotel, once one of New Orleans's finest architectural landmarks. Designed by famed architect J.N. BB. dePouilly and built in 1838, the St. Louis Hotel now exists only in a large painting in the lobby of the Royal Orleans. Even though the financial crisis of 1837 made it necessary to build a much more modest structure than was originally intended, the St. Louis was still lavish by nineteenth century standards, boasting a bank, public baths, and shops. The original building burned in 1841, but a new one was erected on the same site and along the same lines as the original. Slave auctions were held in the lobby beneath the hotel's great copper-plated dome, which weighed 100 tons. One of the patrons who took advantage of the free lunches that were served in the bar during mid-day slave sales was **Walt Whitman**, who visited the hotel in late 1848 and saw his first slave auction there, a spectacle that made a lasting impression on him. In **Harriet Beecher Stowe**'s (1811–1896) novel *Uncle Tom's Cabin,* Uncle Tom is sold in a New Orleans hotel rotunda much like the one in the St. Louis Hotel. When **Mark Twain** visited the St. Louis Hotel in 1882, it had already lost some of its splendor and housed a variety of municipal offices. In *Life on the Mississippi,* Twain said that "if a broom or a shovel has ever been used in it, there is no evidence to back up the fact." In 1915, the St. Louis Hotel was badly damaged by a hurricane and the owners allowed it to fall into disrepair and stand vacant for years. When the British writer and world-traveler **John Galsworthy** (1867–1933) took the "two-bit tour" through the apartments in 1925, he met a white horse in the hallway and wrote a "prose poem" about the event, "That Old Time Place," which was included in his book, *The Inn of Tranquillity.* The hotel was finally demolished.

Antoine's, the restaurant at 713 St. Louis Street, is the oldest continuously operated family-run restaurant in America. Since 1840, Antoine's has served its famed Creole cuisine to many literary celebrities. In 1971, while he was recovering from a severe illness, **Tennessee Williams** dined at Antoine's on Oysters Rockefeller with Oliver Evans and Victor Campbell, a new secretary-companion. In 1951, **William Faulkner** ate dinner here with **Hermann Deutsch**, a New Orleans journalist whose stories were published in *Esquire* and the *Saturday Evening Post.* For dessert, Faulkner was served Antoine's best-known dessert, Baked Alaska, lettered with the words "The Ignoble Prize."

The old four-storied building at 640 Royal Street goes under three names. Because it is probably the first structure more than one story high to be built in the Old Square, it is known by many as the "First Sky-scraper." In its early years, locals avoided this house on stormy days because it was believed that the soft soil would not support such a massive edifice. The building's second name, "Dr. Le Monnier's Resi-dence," is a reference to Dr. Yves Le Monnier, who built the house in 1811. The building's third name, "'Sieur George's House," is taken from the name of **George Washington Cable**'s fictional hero who was ruined by drinking, gambling, and loving the wrong woman.

John James Audubon (1785–1851) lived in the little cottage at 505 Dauphine Street from 1821–22 while working on his collection of paintings published as *Birds of America*. He rented the little house for seventeen dollars a month. Audubon had arrived here from Kentucky, having completed "62 Drawings of Birds & Plants, 3 Quadrupeds, 2 Snakes, 50 Portraits of All Sorts and My Father Dontonio." Audubon also gave private art lessons to wealthy residents such as Mrs. William Brand, wife of a prominent architect. She and her son studied painting with Audubon at her home at 698 Magazine Street. By December 1821, Audubon had made enough money to bring his wife, Lucy, to New Orleans. However, after a few months, Lucy and her children moved from the Dauphine Street cottage because her husband was paying more attention to his birds than he was to them. She moved in with the Brands and became the governess to their son, William. Audubon's *Journal,* which he kept during the winters of 1821 and 1822 reflects the emotional toll that the separation from his family took on him, provides detailed descriptions of life in the city and on the river, and gives the reader some insight into the inner turmoil that was produced from the friction between Audubon the scientist and Audubon the romantic. It also revealed his disdain for the New Orleans social life and laid-back approach to life. The careless errors in grammar, punctuation, and spelling suggest that the journal was written hurriedly.

The intersection of St. Louis and Royal streets was termed by Audubon the "Corner of Events" because of a romantic interlude that he had here during his visit to New Orleans. In 1821, he met a veiled lady who invited him, in French, to paint her likeness in her home at 26 Rue d'Amour, a street where the quadroon mistresses of many prominent Creole men lived. On his first visit, the lady removed her veil, then disappeared behind some curtains, where she removed the rest of her clothes. In his *Journal,* Audubon wrote, "I had the pleasure of this beautiful Woman's company about one hour naked. . . ." Audubon continued to visit the woman's house at the same time every day until the

719 Toulouse Street

portrait was completed. For payment, the lady gave him an engraved "souvenir" hunting rifle, which became one of his prized possessions. Audubon honored her request never to reveal her name.

The little Creole cottage at 719 Toulouse Street was the home of *Times-Picayune* reporter **Roark Bradford**. Bradford eventually ended his career in journalism and pursued fiction writing full-time. He had a reputation for knowing the blacks of the Deep South better than any other writer. His novel *Ol' Man Adam an' His Chillun* was the inspiration for Marc Connelly's Pulitzer-winning play *Green Pastures*. However, like his friend Lyle Saxon, Bradford is best known today as the friend and confidante of writers who enjoyed greater success than his own. Bradford, the "nightside" city desk reporter of the *Times-Picayune,* held parties at his house after getting off work early in the morning. Most of the time, the parties did not get into "full swing" until three o'clock in the morning. Bradford, an expert storyteller, entertained his guests with elaborate stories of his adventures that usually crossed the line into fiction. It is likely that Lyle Saxon influenced Bradford, who was also the Sunday editor of the *Times-Picayune*, to "look up" **William Faulkner** and to publish his series of sketches. Faulkner sold four for twenty dollars. This was the first money that Faulkner had ever received for writing fiction.

Right across the street at 722 Toulouse Street is the house where **Tennessee Williams** lived from 1938 to 1939. He rented the attic room behind the dormer window on the Royal Street side for ten dollars a month from a Mrs. Anderson, whom Williams characterized as "a lovely Mississippi lady." Though his rent was low and food in the Quarter was cheap, Williams had to pawn most of his possessions, including clothes and an old portable typewriter. He hoped to get work with the Federal Writers' Project, but the job never materialized. After Mrs. Anderson converted the townhouse into a restaurant, she hired Williams as a waiter. He promoted his landlady's short-lived venture with cards bearing a motto that he had written: "Meals in the Quarter for a Quarter." The restaurant's failure can be attributed, at least in part, to Mrs. Anderson's bad temper. One night she poured water from her kitchen window on a party being given on the first floor by photographer Joseph G. Patterson. Mrs. Anderson was arrested, and the next day, she, Williams, and some of the guests were summoned to court at the Third Precinct Police Station on Chartres Street. Williams incorporated this incident practically "in toto" in his 1978 play *Vieux Carre*. The water-pouring incident also led to new friendships for Williams. He visited Rose Bradford, one of the party guests who had been soaked, to explain that he had nothing to do with ruining her dress. Through Mrs. Bradford, Williams met a New York producer, Sam Byrd. The Bradfords also introduced Williams to

Lyle Saxon and Olive Leonhardt, an artist whose work is featured in *New Orleans: Drawn and Quartered.*

Years later, Williams said that these formative months in the Toulouse Street townhouse gave him the freedom he needed to become a true artist. The scripts that he mailed from the Toulouse Street address were the first of his plays to bear the name "Tennessee." He also discarded the conservative style that he brought with him to New Orleans in favor of the "bohemian look" of sports shirts and sandals. The "new kind of life" that Williams was exposed to in 1938 and 1939 found its way into his work over the next forty years. Williams claimed that he was forced to escape down a bed-sheet rope on his last day in the apartment because he owed his landlady fifty dollars. However, the Quarter's exotic flavor and diversity brought him back time after time.

Williams referred to the 1960s as the "stoned age," a very unhappy time for the playwright which culminated in a nervous breakdown in 1969. When he returned to New Orleans during this time for brief visits, he stayed at an exclusive guest house called Maison de Ville at 727 Toulouse Street, almost directly across the street from his old apartment house.

The house at 616 St. Peter Street was the home of the first amateur theater in the nation. Le Petit Theatre du Vieux Carre is actually the outgrowth of the Drawing Room Players, organized in 1916, which moved to this location when the group had outgrown its Pontalba apartment. The 500-seat Le Petit Theatre put on plays by well-known playwrights such as **Eugene O'Neill** and by local playwrights such as **Flo Field**. When **Sinclair Lewis** (1885–1951) visited New Orleans in the 1930s, he appeared at Le Petit Theatre in a play entitled *Shadow and Substance.* Lewis was a talented mimic, especially of clergymen, politicians, and other writers. When it appeared that his writing was waning after winning the Nobel Prize in 1930, he decided to capitalize on his ability to impersonate certain types of people and embarked on an acting career in the late 1930s and early 1940s, appearing in summer productions of Eugene O'Neill's *Ah Wilderness!* and **Thornton Wilder**'s *Our Town.*

Le Petit Theatre du Vieux Carre
616 St. Peter Street

The Creole home right next door at 620 St. Peter Street is the original meeting place of Le Petit Salon, a ladies' literary society founded by **Grace King** (1852–1932), the Salon's first president. The club was set up primarily to give the female writers of New Orleans a forum where they could discuss their ideas. Occasionally, well-known writers like **Sherwood Anderson** were featured as guest speakers. Le Petit Salon is still an active women's literary club.

Aunt Rose Arnold, one of New Orleans's most famous madams, lived on Chartres Street next to Le Petit Theatre du Viex Carre. The house was one block west of St. Louis Cathedral and half a block north of Jackson Square, which it faced. Standing more than six feet tall, this red-haired woman projected a motherly persona that persisted into her later years when William Faulkner and Sherwood Anderson were living in the Quarter. She was a generous woman who looked after sailors and itinerant writers. Her "house of ill repute," where she rented rooms to individual girls and to couples seeking a safe rendezvous, thrived even after the closing of Storyville, New Orleans's red-light district, in 1917. The motto on her wall read, "'Don't be a good fellow'—JOHN D.

ROCKEFELLER." Sherwood Anderson immortalized her in his short story "A Meeting South," which portrays the friendship between a retired madam called Aunt Sally and a little Southern man named David, a thinly disguised representation of **William Faulkner**. Faulkner based the character of "Miss Reba" in his last novel, *The Reivers,* on Aunt Rose.

After King's death in 1932, Le Petit Salon was headed by **Elizabeth Meriwether Gilmer** (1861?–1951). Beginning in 1896, Gilmer wrote articles on love and family relationships for the Sunday edition of the *New Orleans Picayune*. She was hired by Elizabeth Nicholson, one of the first female publishers of a large newspaper. Eventually, Gilmer was given her own column. Working under the pseudonym Dorothy Dix, Gilmer become one of the most popular newspaper columnists of her day. She left New Orleans in 1901 to join the staff of William Randolph Hearst's *New York Journal,* which featured "Dorothy Dix Talks" six times per week. Her newspaper career lasted nearly sixty years. She also wrote six books, including *Dorothy Dix—Her Book: Everyday Help for Everyday People* (1926).

The Avaret-Paretti House at 632 St. Peter Street is where **Tennessee Williams** lived from 1946–1947 when he wrote *A Streetcar Named Desire*. He worked in a little room under the third-floor skylight, which afforded him a wonderful view of the clouds which seemed to be so close to the roof that he could touch them. His first project after moving into the townhouse was the play *Summer and Smoke;* however, the indifferent attitude of a young friend toward the play prompted him to resume work on *A Streetcar Named Desire,* which had the working title "The Poker Night." The new title came from the streetcar running up Royal Street that he could see from his window. He also transferred his own address—632—to that of his fictional house on Elysian Fields. Dick Orme, Williams's landlord, read the completed manuscript and is reputed to have said, "Now, Tennessee, you can do better than that." Orme later said that he was referring to the title, not to the play itself.

Williams thoroughly immersed himself in the street life of the French Quarter during the writing of *Streetcar*. After writing until early afternoon, he would walk around the corner to Victor's Restaurant, where he would drink a Brandy Alexander, eat a sandwich, and listen to the jukebox. Williams would then walk over to Rampart Street for a swim at the New Orleans Athletic Club. Sometimes, he would meet **Lorrain Welein Moore** at Jackson Square and talk about his play and the novel that she was working on.

Heading back toward Canal Street on Bourbon, New Orleans's best-known street, one understands how the city got its reputation as a "party town." "The Street," as the locals refer to Bourbon Street, is dotted with a variety of watering holes—jazz bars, piano bars, historic bars, and, of course, the sleazy bars it is famous for. Actually, Bourbon Street is just as well known for the wide spectrum of music that blares from the open doors—Dixieland, Karaoke, Cajun, can-cans, and low-down mean blues (affectionately known as gutbucket). Some of New Orleans's finest restaurants can be found on Bourbon Street. For generations, the denizens of Bourbon Street have appeared in novels, some written by writers who observed the party from a safe distance, others by those who threw themselves body and soul into the frenzied life around them.

The Spanish Colonial mansion at 623 Bourbon is most recently the home of ex-Congresswoman Lindy Boggs, ambassador to the Vatican. However, this stately old home that was built in 1795 was also the home of playwright **Thornton Wilder** for a brief time. Although Wilder is best-known for *Our Town*, set in New England, two of his lesser-known works are set in New Orleans. *Queens of France,* which takes place in the New Orleans of 1869, is a comic piece about a crooked lawyer who cons lonely women into believing they are descended from French royalty. He collects a hefty fee from each of them to conduct a "search" for the documents that would let them claim the title of "Queen of France."

The old house at 516 Bourbon Street was the home of one of New Orleans's most colorful writers, **Lafcadio Hearn** (1850–1904). Born in the Ionian Islands off the west coast of Greece to a British father and Greek mother, he was educated with relatives in England, then immigrated to the United States at age nineteen. In 1877 he moved to New Orleans from Cincinnati, where he had worked for a newspaper, the *Commercial.* He continued to send articles about New Orleans tourist sites and Creole life back to the *Commercial* until January 1878. His initial impressions of the city were tinged with romanticism: "The wealth of the world is here,—unworked gold in the ore, one might say; the paradise of the South is here, deserted and half in ruins. I never beheld anything so beautiful and so sad." Between irregular checks from the *Commercial,* he took odd jobs which barely kept him from starving. Also, he had arrived in time to witness New Orleans's last great yellow fever epidemic. At one point, Hearn thought he had contracted the disease, but he actually had dengue fever. During his entire stay in New Orleans, he was haunted by the fear that he was going blind; he had already lost one eye in a childhood accident. To make matters worse, Hearn was taken advantage of by a series of landladies, who convinced him that the residents of the Quarter were "too evil to live with." His long hair and haggard appearance made him look even worse than the vagrants he befriended. He never got over the feeling that he was being swindled the entire time he was in New Orleans.

Hearn's fortunes improved somewhat when he took a job with the New Orleans *Item.* For three years, he served as chief editorial writer, critic, and even cartoonist. After that, he submitted articles for the *Times Democrat.*

In his early pieces, he condemned police inefficiency, child labor, white slavery, and gang rule. He also argued against women being allowed to smoke or vote. He did much of his writing in his apartments, like the houses at 516 Bourbon Street (now a jazz joint) and 228 Baronne Street (no longer there). From his Bourbon Street apartment, he could see the well-dressed audiences come and go in the Frenchy Opera House across the street. The little man with the swarthy complexion became an easily recognized figure as he walked around Canal, Royal, Bourbon, and Toulouse streets in a broad-brimmed black hat collecting Creole and gypsy folk tales, which he rewrote in the original dialect. Some of these tales appeared in a series of eerie sketches called "Fantastics."

Before long he became known in the intellectual circles. **George Washington Cable**, for example, was interested in the Creole songs that Hearn was recording and invited him to his Eighth Street House. Earlier, Cable had helped Hearn make up his mind to come to New Orleans when Hearn read Cable's short story "Jean-ah Poquelin" in the May 1875 issue of *Scribner's Magazine.* Hearn was so fascinated by Cable's portrayal of Louisiana culture that he wanted to meet the author. Through Cable, Hearn also met **Joel Chandler Harris**, who applauded his attempt to translate Theophile Gautier's writings into English. The Creole poet-priest **Adrien Rouquette** shared Hearn's love of Creole folklore and became a close friend of Hearn. Even the refined **Grace King** was taken with this rough little man. By reading his articles in the *Times-Democrat,* she learned to use French writers as models for her own fiction. Eventually, Hearn moved to 278 Canal Street to be nearer to a dining room and boarding house run by kindly Mrs. Courtney at 68 Gasquet Street, a few blocks from the Louisiana Medical University which later became the Tulane University Medical School. Thanks to her good food and friendship, Hearn gained weight and adopted a more positive attitude toward the city. He wrote **H. E. Krehbile**, music editor of the *New York Tribune,* that he would rather be in New Orleans in sackcloth and ashes than to own the whole state of Ohio.

Hearn left the United States in 1890 to do a series of articles on Japan for *Harper's New Monthly* and ended up staying there the rest of his life. He married a samurai woman and became a Japanese subject, writing under the name Yakumo Koizumi. His collections of supernatural tales collected in such works as *Some Chinese Ghosts* (1887) turned him into something of a Japanese national hero. Ironically, he is all but forgotten in the U.S., partially because his romantic style was becoming antiquated even at the time he was writing. However, Hearn's *Chita* is now considered one of the classics of Louisiana literature. He suffered a fatal heart attack in 1904 and his ashes are buried in a Buddhist cemetery in Japan.

Not much is known about **O. Henry's** brief stay in New Orleans in 1894, primarily because he was hiding out to avoid being jailed on embezzlement charges in Austin, Texas, and he did not want to advertise his whereabouts. However, one of his letters reveals that he lived in "a dim *chambre garnie* in Bienville Street," which was across the street from the Old Absinthe House at 238 Bourbon Street. This structure, built in 1806, is a typical *entresol,* or mezzanine, house. In the nineteenth century, traders, adventurers, and Creole gentlemen congregated here to drink absinthe. According to legend, General Andrew Jackson and Jean Lafitte planned the defense of New Orleans in a secret chamber on second floor of this old building. O. Henry's room on Bienville Street was near Madame Louis Beguet's restaurant. While living in this area, O. Henry wrote coded notes to his wife, Athol. To prevent the authorities from tracing him back to New Orleans, most of his notes took the form of unsigned drawings, such as a picture of a woman holding a baby and looking across the river at a man who stood with his arms outstretched and tears running down his face. When O. Henry left New Orleans to travel to Honduras, he sent his wife a sketch of two hands clasped as if shaking good-bye. In the background was a sailing vessel, indicating that he was going to Central America.

Galatoire's at 209 Bourbon Street is another of New Orleans's old-line French Creole restaurants. Founded at the turn of the century, this 140-seat restaurant is renowned for its sophisticated fare and extensive menu. Many writers have dined here when they could afford to. **William Faulkner** threw a party here in the early 1930s after receiving a check for an advance against royalties for the publication of his novel *Mosquitoes*. The check had been sent to him by Lillian Hellman, who was working as a reader for Horace Liveright at the time. Faulkner did not own the proper attire for Galatoires, so his friends had to obtain a coat and tie for him and force him to wear them. Galatoires was **Tennessee Williams**'s favorite restaurant; he ate here frequently during his affluent years. **Walker Percy** also loved to dine here. His friend **Sheila Bosworth** (1950–) used him in her novel *Almost Innocent* as the model for the writer from Covington who dines at Galatoire's. Bosworth was a member of the Sons and Daughters of the Apocalypse, Percy's lunch group that met at Bechac's restaurant in Mandeville. In 1984, Percy agreed to read the first fifty pages of Bosworth's novel; afterwards, he asked her husband if he would mind if he gave Sheila a hug. Bosworth also served as the Percys' unofficial fashion consultant. Before flying to Rome for an audience with the Pope, Percy asked Bosworth what his wife should wear. Percy said that he shouldn't be expected to know Vatican protocol because he was just a convert to Catholicism.

On the outskirts of the French Quarter at 400 Basin Street between Conti and St. Louis Streets is St. Louis Cemetery No. 1, the oldest cemetery in New Orleans. **Mark Twain** (1835–1910) was thinking of this cemetery and the city's other above-ground graveyards when he observed in *Life on the Mississippi* that "there is no architecture in New Orleans, except in the cemeteries." He was struck by the vaults' "resemblance to houses—sometimes to temples . . . and when one walks through the midst of a thousand or so of them, and sees their white roofs and gables stretching into the distance on every hand, the phrase 'city of the dead' has all at once a meaning to him." This venerable old cemetery, which is still in use, displays all of the effects of the passing of the years and neglect. The tomb of the cemetery's most famous occupant, "voodoo queen" Marie Leveau, has, like many others, fallen prey to time and vandalism. The tomb is covered with X's, put there by visitors for good luck. St. Louis Cemetery No. 1 appears in more of **Anne Rice**'s novels than any other cemetery. For example, in *Interview with a Vampire,* Louis says that his brother is buried here. Rice's personal attachment to this cemetery has earned her a fake deed to a plot. **Walker Percy** also has a connection to St. Louis Cemetery No. 1: he was a pallbearer here in the 1960s.

The Riverfront

The mighty Mississippi River that flows through New Orleans may look and smell the same as in the days of Audubon, Twain, and Whitman, but the sailors, tradesmen, and wharf rats who populated the 19th century Riverfront District have been replaced by wide-eyed tourists with cameras slung over their shoulders. The Moon Walk, a wooden walkway named for former mayor Moon Landrieu, lets visitors walk safely right down to the water's edge, and provides a spectacular view of the tugs, barges, ferries, and huge freighters that make up the traffic on the still-busy river. Several authentic-looking riverboats, complete with huge paddlewheels, dock along this stretch of the river and can be boarded for cruises. Replicas of the famous New Orleans streetcars (including one labeled Desire) roll along tracks parallel to the river and provide convenient access to the New Orleans Aquarium and to nearby Jax Brewery, a historic beer manufacturing plant that was converted in 1984 to a festival marketplace. The brewery is on the river side of Decatur at St. Peter Street. By walking down Decatur, which cuts between Jackson Square and the Riverfront, visitors can sample New Orleans cuisine at numerous delis and coffeehouses. The most famous restaurant on the Riverfront is the Cafe du Monde, an open-air pavilion at the corner of St. Ann and Decatur, whose freshly baked beignets have been known to attract writers such as Tennessee Williams. For more than a century, writers and artists have joined locals and tourists to start their day with *beignets* and *cafe au lait* at the Cafe du Monde. Tap dancers, sketch artists, mimes, and other street performers can be seen in Jackson Square and across Decatur from Jackson Square at Washington Artillery Park.

Jackson Square is considered by many to be the "heart" of New Orleans. **Mark Twain** (1835–1910) said that Jackson Square was

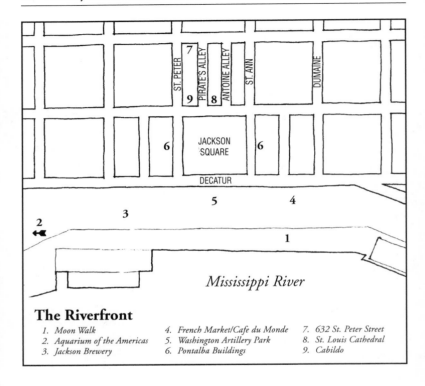

The Riverfront

1. *Moon Walk*
2. *Aquarium of the Americas*
3. *Jackson Brewery*
4. *French Market/Cafe du Monde*
5. *Washington Artillery Park*
6. *Pontalba Buildings*
7. *632 St. Peter Street*
8. *St. Louis Cathedral*
9. *Cabildo*

"brilliant with a worldly sort [of light]," a reference to the free-spirited activity that still goes on there. Situated directly in front of St. Louis Cathedral, Jackson Square is bordered by St. Ann, St. Peter, Chartres, and Decatur streets. The Square was originally named the Place d'Armes, and many flags have floated from its flagstaffs in the two hundred plus years that have passed. The centerpiece of the Square today is the famous statue of Andrew Jackson, hero of the 1812 Battle of New Orleans.

After being ordered to stand trial for the embezzlement of funds from the First National Bank of Austin, Texas, short-story writer

Jackson Square

O. Henry (William Sidney Porter) (1862–1910) stopped off at New Orleans on his way to Honduras, where he planned to get a new start in life. He helped make ends meet by writing for local newspapers like the *New Orleans,* the *Delta,* and the *Picayune.* While strolling around Jackson Square, the "little, iron-railed park of flowers and immaculate gravelled walks, where citizens take the air of evenings," Porter absorbed the Creole dialect and found the models for characters that appeared in such later stories as "Hostages to Momus," "Blind Man's Holiday," "Cherchez la Femme," "Whistling Dick's Christmas Stocking," and "The Renaissance at Charleroi." He also claimed that he first started using the pen name O. Henry while he was in New Orleans. According to legend, he was drinking in a bar near the New Orleans *Item* when he said that he was looking for a pen name for the short stories he was writing. Suddenly, someone yelled to the bartender, "Oh, Henry! Another of the same!" One of his drinking buddies immediately responded with, "There's your pseudonym!"

The mourners who had attended **Tennessee Williams**'s memorial service congregated here afterwards and shared their memories of him. In 1945, a young **Truman Capote** (1924–1984) attempted to supplement the small income he was receiving from his father by selling paintings to tourists in Jackson Square. Even he admitted that his paintings were terrible, and he soon gave up and left for New York.

A frequent visitor to Jackson Square was **Sherwood Anderson** (1876–1941), who lived in the Pontalba Buildings lining St. Anne and St. Peter streets along the south side of the Square between 1922–1925. During this period, Anderson wrote a series of impressionistic studies called "New Testament." His short story about New Orleans, "A Meeting South," originally published in the *Dial,* and articles first printed in the *Double Dealer,* a local magazine, were included in his book, *Sherwood Anderson's Notebook.* The *Double Dealer,* named after the play by William

Congreve, was founded by Julius Weis Friend and Albert Goldstein in 1920 at 204 Baronne Street and featured works by **Hart Crane**, **John Crowe Ransom**, **Allen Tate**, **Robert Penn Warren**, and **Thornton Wilder**.

When he arrived in New Orleans, Anderson liked it so much that he wrote an article for the *Double Dealer* entitled "New Orleans, the *Double Dealer* and the Modern Movement in America." In this article, Anderson promoted New Orleans, particularly the French Quarter, as a haven for up-and-coming writers and artists. Consequently, Anderson's apartment became the gathering place for young and established writers, many of whom ate dinner every Saturday night with Sherwood and his wife Elizabeth. His guest list includes such notable writers as **Booth Tarkington** (1869–1946), **W. Somerset Maugham** (1874–1965), **Eugene Field**, and **Edna St. Vincent Millay** (1892–1950). An accomplished raconteur, Anderson enchanted his guests with his ability to "illuminate the commonplace and endow it with significance." Author and critic **Edmund Wilson** (1895–1972) made Anderson's acquaintance in New Orleans in 1926. Anderson and Wilson were very fond of each other, although Anderson was somewhat taken aback by Wilson's extremely mental approach to life. While in New Orleans, Wilson, just recently separated from Mary Blair, had sex with a prostitute who, he said, threw herself on the bed and pulled her skirts up over her stomach.

Anderson wrote an essay about one of his famous guests, sportswriter and short-story writer **Ring Lardner** (1855–1933). Lardner and his wife stopped off at the Pontalba Buildings on a trip that took them to Florida, New Orleans, and California. Lardner was turned off by the "stupid morons" who were celebrating Mardi Gras and by the fashionable bores at an exclusive club who professed their admiration for him. He quickly repelled one of these snobbish New Orleanians with the admission that he was born in Niles, Michigan, of "colored parents." To help Lardner escape these pretentious people, Anderson arranged a dinner party at a small French restaurant for the visiting couple. Anderson reported in his article that Lardner's warm affection for everyone in the restaurant was so evident that two years later, the French chef poured Anderson a glass of wine and toasted "that man you brought here that time . . . to Ring Lardner." However, Anderson's essay contained the admission that he thought Lardner had "smeared" his talent by catering to the masses.

Anderson's most famous protégé during this period was **William Faulkner** (1897–1962), who first met Anderson at his Pontalba apartment in 1924. It is said that Faulkner was so fond of Anderson's apartment that Mrs. Anderson suggested to her husband that he find the young writer another place to stay. At this time, Faulkner was a young man who had not yet reached his peak, while Anderson was declining from the summit of his career. Still, Faulkner learned much from his afternoon and evening meetings with the master, during which both men would drink and Anderson would talk. Faulkner recalled finding Anderson seated on a bench in Jackson Square one day, laughing about a dream in which he had walked up and down country roads in an attempt to swap a horse for a night's sleep. Faulkner believed that this story was not a dream but a symbolic representation of Anderson's view of the American dream.

Just west of the Pontalba Building down Cabildo Alley, also known as Pirate's Alley, is the place where Faulkner lived from 1925–1926. The apartment building at 632 St. Peter Street, almost at the corner of Cabildo Alley, was leased by Marc and Lucille Antony. Their gallery and shop were on the first floor; they lived on the third floor. The first floor of this building is now occupied by a bookstore, Faulkner House Books. A plaque outside the bookstore announces that "Here in 1925 William Faulkner, Nobel Laureate, wrote his first novel, *Soldier's Pay*." Faulkner and his friend **William Spratling** (1900–1967) lived in the attic.

Pirate's Alley

Spratling, a dour 24-year-old with a dark brown mustache, taught architecture at Tulane University. With Faulkner, Spratling compiled 41 sketches of people he had met in the Quarter into a book entitled *Sherwood Anderson & Other Famous Creoles*. Faulkner provided the text as well as a 500-word "foreword," which was a parody of Anderson's writing style. Their book was dedicated "To All the Artful and Crafty Ones of the French Quarter." On the cover was a drawing of the view from St. Peter Street and Cabildo Alley. A figure who bore a striking resemblance to Faulkner himself was pictured leaning out of a fourth-floor window. This publication had a decidedly cooling effect on Faulkner's relationship with Anderson.

Because Spratling shared Faulkner's love for nightlife, their apartment was the site of frequent parties where other young, aspiring writers talked, smoked, and drank liquor from a big bowl on the table. Sometimes, the guests drank bottles of pernod made by a Swiss living in the Quarter; at other times, Faulkner and Spratling served homemade gin they had aerated by rolling a barrel across the floor to the chagrin of the tenants who lived below, who were also perturbed by Faulkner's habit of typing articles late at night for the *Double Dealer* and the *Times-Picayune*.

One of their guests was **Oliver LaFarge** (1901–1963), who enjoyed talking about the Southwest while wearing an Indian headband. He also entertained his listeners by jumping up on tables and performing his rendition of the "Eagle Dance." One night, LaFarge dropped a dozen of the Antonys' expensive glasses out of the dormer window, one by one. During an even wilder party, Faulkner initiated a game of tag across the steeply angled roofs of the Quarter. On rainy days, the two men amused themselves by aiming their Daisy air rifle through the windows that overlooked St. Peters Street and shooting passersby in the buttocks. Spratling had fond memories of shooting the broad backside of a wealthy dowager as she was exiting her limousine.

Faulkner often went in the mornings, usually after a hard night's partying, to a coffee stand in the French Market on the corner of Decatur and Dumaine. New Orleans writer **Flo Field** recalled seeing Faulkner returning to his apartment one morning with three powdered donuts which he washed down with a tumbler of whiskey. Another young woman who was shocked by Faulkner's constant drinking was **Anita Loos** (1893–1981). She had been visiting the Andersons with her actor-director husband, John Emerson, who had known Sherwood since childhood. Loos recalled Faulkner stumbling down the stairs one morning holding a glass of what she was certain was corn liquor. Later, she and Faulkner climbed the stone steps of the tower of the St. Louis Cathedral and entered the belfry, where Faulkner purchased liquor from a young priest. Like most of the writers who met Faulkner in New Orleans, she believed that he had been a war hero in World War I and that one could not "expect much from Bill" because of a steel plate that he was supposed to have in his head.

The French Market was visited by other writers as well. It consists of seven structures, the oldest of which is the Meat Market, built in 1813. It has housed the Cafe du Monde since the early 1860s. Destroyed by a hurricane, the Market was rebuilt as seen today in the late 1930s. **John**

St. Louis Cathedral

James Audubon scoured the French Market at dawn one day in 1821 for various birds that were offered for sale, such as mallards, Canadian geese, bluebirds, and red-winged starlings. However, he did not buy any because they were too expensive. Instead, he shot his own birds in and around New Orleans and used them as his models for *Birds of America*. **Walt Whitman** (1819–1892) went to the French Market to take in the different dialects and to buy a large cup of coffee from a 230-pound mulatto woman. When she was barely a teenager, **Lillian Hellman** was approached in the French Market by an old man who exposed himself.

Facing the Square on Cathedral Street is the stately St. Louis Cathedral, named for the patron saint of Bourbon France and of Nouvelle Orleans. The Cathedral has made a lasting impression on writers down through the centuries. **Mark Twain** said that the Cathedral was "dim with a religious light." **O. Henry** referred to the imposing structure as a "provincial ghost." **Lillian Hellman** recalled running away from home for 48 hours after getting into an argument with her father over the identity of a boyfriend, a lock of whose hair she had placed in the back of a new watch. Distraught at the indignities she had suffered at the hands of the low-lifes in the red-light section of Bourbon Street, Hellman went to sleep behind a bush in Jackson Square. Rudely awakened by two rats, she screamed and pounded on the doors of the St. Louis Cathedral in a vain attempt to find a place to spend the night. Eventually, her father found her and took her home. **Tennessee Williams** enjoyed visiting the Cathedral because it made him feel he was in a theater. Williams added that had he been around the Cathedral all of the time, he might have gone to confession on a regular basis. He was memorialized at St. Louis Cathedral on March 19, 1983, and the bells that he made to ring in *A Streetcar Named Desire* were rung in his honor. In **Anne Rice**'s novel *Interview with a Vampire,* Louis drained the blood from the throat of a priest at the Cathedral's communion railing.

The Cabildo

To the left of the cathedral at 701 Chartres is the Cabildo, the seat of Spanish rule. Construction began in 1795 and continued until 1803. The Louisiana Purchase was signed in the Sala Capitular on the second floor of the Cabildo before construction was completed. **O. Henry** said that in the Cabildo, "Spanish justice fell like hail." When Lafayette visited New Orleans in 1825, he resided in the Cabildo for a week. Other famous people received there include Henry Clay, Sarah Bernhardt, Grand Duke Alexis of Russia, **Mark Twain**, Theodore Roosevelt, William McKinley, and William Howard Taft. The roof and top floor of the Cabildo were severely damaged by fire in 1988, but fully restored in 1994.

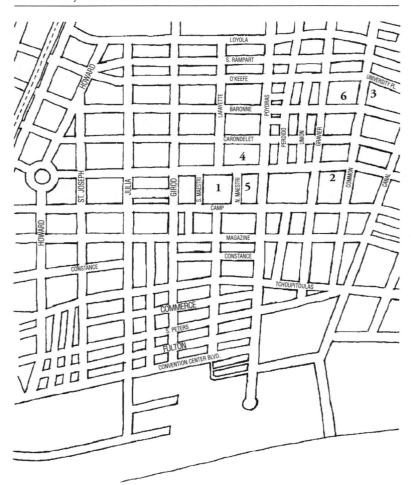

The Central Business District

1. *Lafayette Square*
2. *Place de St. Charles*
3. *The Fairmont Hotel (The Roosevelt)*
4. *534 St. Charles Avenue (Gallier Hall)*
5. *615 North Maestri Street (Times-Picayune)*
6. *228 Baronne Street*

The Central Business District

The Central Business District occupies land owned by the Jesuits before their expulsion in 1763. Afterwards, the land was bought by Gernard Gravier, who parceled the plantation into lots and developed the city's first suburb. By the 1830s, Anglo-Americans had taken over the suburb, which subsequently became known as the American section. A wide stretch of land on which a canal was to be built was the median between the American Section and the French Quarter. The canal was never built, and the median became Canal Street, the "neutral ground." The Central Business District (called by locals, the CBD) is also bordered by Loyola Avenue, Howard Avenue, and the Mississippi River. In contrast to the Garden District or the French Quarter, the CBD appears contemporary. The area is filled with ultramodern buildings such as the Superdome and several high-rise convention hotels. But even this newer section of New Orleans has a literary tradition.

The CBD's most illustrious literary occupant was undoubtedly **Walt Whitman** (1819–1892). He arrived in New Orleans from Brooklyn after a dispute with the editor, Van Anden, over the Wilmot Proviso, which Whitman supported. From March to May, 1848, Whitman worked, with his brother Jeff, as assistant editor of the *Daily Crescent* newspaper at 93 St. Charles Street. The brothers Whitman found a room in a boarding house at the corner of Tojdrass Street and St. Charles, but left because it was so squalid. They soon found a better apartment for nine dollars a week just around the corner at the Tremont House. Jeff was hired at the *Daily Crescent* for five dollars a week as office boy and printer's devil, while Whitman's job was to coordinate the activities of his staff of three men and to oversee the layout. Because the newspaper was such a small enterprise, he had to perform menial tasks as well, such as carrying the outgoing mail bags, which he complained were too heavy. Whitman earned extra money by writing features, a job that took him out on the streets to interview such colorful characters as a flower girl/streetwalker, a con man, and an oyster vendor. The resulting sketches were written in a mixture of slang and prose, which became one of his poetic trademarks. Interestingly, Whitman avoided controversial political issues in his articles, probably because his anti-slavery views would jeopardize his job in a town where slave auctions were a common sight. Whitman's short stay in New Orleans was not altogether pleasant. He contracted dysentery, and his brother was constantly homesick. They finally left New Orleans on May 27 after Whitman argued with the management of the *Daily Crescent* over money.

Little is known about this period in Whitman's life, during which he wandered from city to city and from newspaper to newspaper; consequently, some aspects of his life in New Orleans are shrouded in mystery, especially his love life. A letter published after his death suggests that while in New Orleans he may have had an intimate relationship with a woman that produced a child, but this has never been confirmed. It is more likely that this romance was with a man, although in old age, Whitman did recall the beauty of the octoroon [women] "with the splendid bodies . . . splendid is too weak a word to apply to them." Something did happen to Whitman in New Orleans, though, that stimulated his poetic impulse. His poem "I Saw in Louisiana a Live Oak Growing" reveals nothing about his experiences in New Orleans, but it does show his desire to be loved for himself so that he too could come into full bloom, like a tree. His travels through Pennsylvania and Virginia, across the Alleghenies, and down the Ohio and Mississippi rivers exposed him for the first time to the vastness of the American landscape, which became a sort of "character" in his epic poem *Leaves of Grass*. In spite of some of the negative experiences Whitman had in New

Orleans, his short time there bred within him a deep sympathy for the South.

Whitman's apartment was not far from Lafayette Square. Bounded by Camp, North and South Maestri, and St. Charles streets, Lafayette Square was the American counterpart of the Creole Place d'Armes (Jackson Square). This is one of the New Orleans sites that Whitman strolled through, ostensibly to collect material for articles. Whitman probably enjoyed indulging his senses in the city's exotic atmosphere and rubbing elbows with the different nationalities that populated the parks and cafes.

The St. Charles Hotel has the oldest literary legacy of any building in New Orleans. The original hotel at 211 St. Charles Street opened in 1837. Its high dome was the first New Orleans landmark seen by many travelers to the city. A new hotel was built on this site after the original burned in 1851. Its guest list included John Wilkes Booth and Jefferson Davis. That second hotel was also destroyed by fire and a third was built on this site in 1896. Although not as grand as its two predecessors, the third incarnation was the site of Mardi Gras balls and debutante balls for over sixty years. It was demolished in 1974, and a new hotel, the Place de St. Charles, was built on the site. **Walt Whitman** sat in the original hotel's smoky barroom sipping "cobblers," brandy, and champagne and talking to potential subjects for his daily sketches in the *Crescent:* the dandy obsessed with following the latest trends, the gentleman whiling away his time racing his horses, the theater manager demonstrating his limited intellect through his innocuous comments. British novelist **William Makepeace Thackery** (1811–1863) was a guest at the St. Charles Hotel during his visit to the city in the 1850s. Thackery, best known for his novel *Vanity Fair,* wrote about his New Orleans experiences in a book entitled *The Roundabout Papers* (1856). His primary concern while in the city seems to have been the quality of its spirits. He found the claret in New Orleans to be of particularly good quality, but all of the liquor served in the city was good, even the "half-dollar Medoc of the public hotel table." The landlord of the St. Charles Hotel made a big impression on Thackery by placing two bottles of the finest Cognac in the writer's stateroom.

It was **Lyle Saxon**, though, who single-handedly turned the St. Charles Hotel into a mecca for writers in the 1930s. Saxon directed the New Orleans literary scene from his suite on the fifth floor. Saxon was drinking up to a fifth a day at this time, served by Joe Gilmore, who was originally hired as a masseuse but ended up serving as butler, yard man, and bartender. Saxon ran a "democratic" salon where a black porter might engage in casual conversation with a cowboy movie star. His writing took a back seat to entertaining during this time, and from 1939 until his death, he wrote very little. His most notable work of this period was *Gumbo Ya Ya,* a collection of folklore edited with Edward Dreyer and Robert Tallant.

The first thing that caught the eye of the casual visitor to Saxon's suite was the expensive furnishings, especially the antique furniture and artwork. **John Dos Passos** (1896–1970) could not take his eyes off an avant-garde painting of Cupid, which he swore was a portrait of Saxon's appendix. **Sinclair Lewis** (1885–1951) probably met Saxon when he stayed at the hotel in October 1939. Saxon had arranged for a friend and associate at the *Times Picayune,* Elizabeth Kell, to interview Lewis in his suite. Saxon and his guests had expected **Dorothy Parker**'s (1893–1967) biting wit to surface during her visit to his suite at the St. Charles; Joe Gilmore was visibly disappointed when Parker came and went without uttering even a negative word to his boss. In the semi-autobiographical *The Friends of Joe Gilmore,* Saxon recounted his helper's impressions of the people who visited the fifth-floor suite in the 1930s and 1940s. Saxon's salon began to wane in 1944 when his bout with cancer required that he make frequent visits to Baptist Hospital in New Orleans. He died in 1946.

Another famous New Orleans hotel, the Roosevelt, exists today at University Place across Canal Street as the Fairmont Hotel. This venerable building has large, lavish suites, the type of accommodations one would expect to find in a grand hotel that has hosted eight U.S. presidents—from Coolidge to Ford—as well as royalty and prime ministers. **Thomas Wolfe** (1900–1938) loved to travel and had come to New Orleans as a boy with his mother. Soon after the publication of his novel *Of Time and the River* in 1935, he returned to New Orleans and stayed at the Roosevelt. He had intended to take a break from writing in New Orleans, but when word leaked out that he had arrived, he got no rest at all. He endeared himself to reporters and admirers with a self-deprecating manner manifest in statements like "if I become an established writer." On his last day in New Orleans, he treated himself to a hearty meal of shrimp remoulade, bouillabaisse, and a Graves at Arnaud's. A man sitting nearby invited himself to sit at Wolfe's table and proceeded to talk to him about literature. Wolfe expressed his admiration for Jesse Stuart and William Saroyan, who would "go places if only he would get that fellow Saroyan out of his writing."

Gallier Hall at 534 St. Charles Avenue, built between 1845 and 1850, may be the most beautiful example of Greek Revival architecture in New Orleans and is probably the most important work of local architect James Gallier Jr. Mardi Gras enthusiasts know this as the place where the King of Carnival toasts with the mayor each year. **Tennessee Williams** was here in September 1973 for a celebration shortly after the St. Charles streetcar line was listed in the National Register of Historical Landmarks. The party was hosted by the Louisiana Landmarks Society and Williams attended with an old friend, Pancho Rodriguez. Another friend who was present was Anna May Maylie, who had known Williams

since the 1940s when he began patronizing Maylie's, a Creole restaurant that she ran with her husband. Maylie said that when she walked into the room in Gallier Hall where the party was being held, Williams came up to her and said, "Come on and dance with me, Anna May. All these [expletive] women want my autograph."

The only surviving daily newspaper in New Orleans, the *Times-Picayune* at 615 North Maestri Street, has had many contributors who went on to make significant contributions to literature. **George Washington Cable, Lafcadio Hearn, Lyle Saxon, O. Henry, Mollie Moore Davis,** and **Pearl Rivers** all wrote for the newspapers that through various mergers evolved into the *Times-Picayune.* **James Conway** (1941–) got his start as a cub reporter for the newspaper between 1965 and 1966. Before long, he was promoted to crime reporter, a job that took him through the Dryades Street slums. Years later in his book *Memphis Afternoons,* Conaway wrote that taking the bus "past black faces and white touched with open, sweet corruption," he was exposed to a side of life that he had never encountered before. Many of the characters he met as a crime reporter appeared in his novel *The Big Easy*.

Jack Kerouac (1922–1969), a leader of the beat movement of the 1950s and 1960s, visited New Orleans in 1944. At the time, Kerouac was in love with a girl named Edie Parker. He wanted her to move in with him, but his mother disapproved. Confused and frustrated, Kerouac took a bus to New Orleans with the intention of rejoining the merchant marine, but was turned down. Left with nothing to do, he got drunk at the N.M.U. hall. He also walked up and down Magazine Street in a failed attempt to strike up a relationship with a lunch-cart waitress. After he ran out of money, he wrote home for bus fare back to New York.

Convinced that something was closing in on him, Kerouac returned to New Orleans in 1949 to visit **William Burroughs** (1914–1997). Kerouac had been unable to find a publisher, and he was having a recurring nightmare of a strange Arab pursuing him relentlessly across the desert. The trip that Kerouac and **Neal Cassady** took from the East Coast to San Francisco by way of the Burroughs household in New Orleans is the first trip recounted in *On the Road*. The two men made the trip fueled by alcohol, marijuana, morphine, and alcohol. Burroughs and his wife, Joan, lived across the Mississippi River from New Orleans in Algiers, Louisiana, at 509 Wagner Street. Burroughs moved here after an abortive attempt to sell his homegrown marijuana in New York, where he once again became addicted to heroin. He took the ferry across the Mississippi every day to the "junk neighborhoods" around Lee Circle and Exchange Place which reminded him of the Time Square drug scene. Heroin in New Orleans was expensive—two dollars a cap—so he had to begin pushing heroin to support his six-caps-a-day habit. The next year, Burroughs began writing about his drug addiction in *Junky*. Burroughs felt that Kerouac's and Cassady's trip was pointless, and he refused to give them a $25 loan to get them to San Francisco. In desperation, Kerouac wired his mother, asking her to dip into his savings account and send him the money so he and Cassady could continue on to the West Coast in their Hudson.

One of the first places **Lafcadio Hearn** (1850–1904) lived when he first moved to New Orleans in 1878 was at 228 Baronne Street. Soon after taking residence here, Hearn sent a postcard to his friend and former employer in Cincinnati, Henry Watkin. Below a sketch he had made of a raven standing at the entrance of the house, he wrote, "Raven liveth at 228 Baronne St. Indite him an epistle. Don't give him particular H—." Hearn was referring to a self-pitying message that he had mailed to Watkin from Memphis, despite the printer's warning to the young man not to let his emotional side rule his life. During the 1930s, this building was used as a tire shop.

Further Reading

Blottner, Joseph. *Faulkner: A Biography.* New York: Random House, 1974.

Bush, Robert. *Grace King: A Southern Destiny.* Baton Rouge: Louisiana State University Press, 1983.

Callow, Philip. *From Noon to Starry Night: A Life of Walt Whitman.* Chicago: Ivan R. Dee, Inc., 1992.

Charters, Ann. *Kerouac: A Biography.* San Francisco: Straight Arrow Books, 1973.

Cherkorski, Hank. *The Life of Charles Bukowski.* New York: Random House, 1991.

Clark, Gerald. *Capote: A Biography.* New York: Simon and Schuster, 1988.

Dickinson, Joy. *Haunted City: An Unauthorized Guide to the Magical, Magnificent New Orleans of Anne Rice.* New York: Citadel Press, 1995.

Federal Writers Project. *The W.P.A. Guide to New Orleans.* New York: Pantheon Books, 1983.

Givner, Joan, *Katherine Anne Porter: A Life.* New York: Simon and Schuster, 1982.

Harvey, Cathy Chance. *Lyle Saxon: A Portrait in Letters, 1917–1947.* Microfilms International, 1980.

Holditch, Kenneth. *In Old New Orleans.* University, MS: University Press of Mississippi, 1983.

_____. "The Last Frontier of Bohemia: Tennessee Williams in New Orleans, 1938-1983." *Southern Quarterly* 23 (1985): 1–37.

King, Grace. *Memories of a Southern Woman of Letters.* New York: Macmillan Co., 1932.

Langford, Gerald. *Alias O. Henry.* New York: Macmillan, 1957.

LeMaster, J. R. and James D. Wilson, eds. *The Mark Twain Encyclopedia.* New York: Garland Publishing, Inc., 1993.

Ludington, Townsend. *John Dos Passos.* New York: E.P. Dutton, 1980.

McWilliams, Vera. *Lafcadio Hearn.* New York; Cooper Square Publishers, Inc., 1970.

Miller, John, ed. *New Orleans Stories.* San Francisco: Chronicle Books, 1992.

Morgan, Ted. *Literary Outlaw: The Life and Times of William S. Burroughs.* New York: Henry Holt & Co., 1985.

Paine, Albert Bigelow. *Mark Twain: A Biography.* New York: Harper and Brothers Publishers, 1912.

Piper, Henry Dan. *F. Scott Fitzgerald: A Critical Portrait.* Carbondale, Ill.: Southern Illinois University Press, 1968.

Spratling, William and William Faulkner. *Sherwood Anderson and Other Famous Creoles.* Austin: University of Texas Press, 1966.

Stevenson, Elizabeth. *Lafcadio Hearn.* New York: The Macmillan Company, 1961.

Thomas, James W. *Lyle Saxon: A Critical Biography.* Birmingham, Ala.: Summa Publications, Inc., 1991.

Tolson, Jay. *Pilgrim in the Ruins: A Life of Walker Percy.* Chapel Hill: University of North Carolina Press, 1992.

Toth, Emily. *Kate Chopin.* New York: William Morrow and Co., 1990.

Townsend, Kim. *Sherwood Anderson: A Biography.* Boston: Houghton Mifflin, 1987.

Turner, Arlin. *George W. Cable: A Biography.* Durham, N.C.: Duke University Press, 1956.

Twain, Mark. *Life on the Mississippi.* New York: Bantam, 1981.

Williams, Tennessee. *Memoirs.* Garden City, N.Y.: Doubleday, 1975.

Wright, William. *Lillian Hellman: The Woman, The Image.* New York: Simon and Schuster, 1986.

Zenfell, Martha. *Insight Guides: New Orleans.* Boston: Houghton Mifflin, 1994.

Index

A

Algren, Nelson 24
Anderson, Sherwood 22, 25, 47, 48, 58–61, 62
Antoine's 42
Armstrong, Louis 7
Armstrong Park. *See* Beauregard Square
Arnold, Rose 47
Audubon, John James 29–30, 42–44, 62
Audubon Park 17–18
Avaret-Paretti House 48

B

Basso, Hamilton 38
Beach, Rex 28
Beauregard Square 25
Beauregard-Keyes House 28
Begue Restaurant 36
Bixby, Horace 12
Bosworth, Sheila 53
Bourbon Street 7, 49
Bradford, Roark 39, 44–45
Brevard House 9
Bristow, Gwen 39
Brooks, Cleanth 17
Bukowski, Charles 31–33

Bultman House 19
Burroughs, William 73–74

C

Cabildo 65
Cable, George Washington 9–12, 12, 13, 33, 35, 38, 42, 51, 72
Cafe du Monde 55, 62
Capote, Truman 31, 35, 58
Carmer, Carl 40
Cassady, Neal 73
Chagall, Claude 14
Chevalier, Maurice 14
Chopin, Kate 18–19, 25, 35
Churchill, Winston 40
Clemens, Samuel. *See* Mark Twain
Conway, James 72
Court of Two Lions 40
Court of Two Sisters 40
Crane, Hart 59

D

Daily Crescent 67–68
Daily Picayune 35
Davis, Mollie E. Moore 35–36
Davis, Mollie Moore 72
dePouilly, J.N. BB. 41
Deutsch, Hermann 42
Dos Passos, John 30–31, 70

Double Dealer 61
Dr. Le Monnier's Residence. *See* 'Sieur George's House
Dreyer, Edward 27, 70

F

Fairmont Hotel. *See* Roosevelt Hotel
Faulkner House Books 60
Faulkner, William 7, 13, 14, 22, 38, 42, 45, 53, 60–61
Field, Eugene 23, 36, 59
Field, Flo 13, 46, 62
First National Bank of Commerce Building. *See* St. Louis Hotel
Fitzgerald, Zelda Sayre 19
Fitzgerald, F. Scott 19
French Market 24, 62–64

G

Galatoire's 53
Gallier Hall 71
Galsworthy, John 42
Gilchrist, Ellen 18
Gilder, Richard Watson 13
Gilmer, Elizabeth Meriwether 48
Gilmore, Joe 25, 70–71

Girod, Nicholas 24
Grau, Shirley Ann 16–17, 29
Gravier, Gernard 67

H

Harris, Joel Chandler 11, 33, 51
Hearn, Lafcadio 11, 50–52, 72, 74
Hellman, Lillian 20–21, 64
Howe, Julia Ward 13
Husband, John 29

I

Item 50

J

Jackson, Andrew 7, 52
Jackson Square 6, 23, 55–58
Jax Brewery 55

K

Kerouac, Jack 73–74
Keyes, Frances Parkinson 28
King, Grace 13–14, 24, 47, 51
Krehbile, H. E. 51

L

La Farge, Oliver 38
Lafayette Cemetery No. 1 19

Lafitte, Jean 7, 52
Lafitte's Blacksmith Shop 31
Lardner, Ring 59–60
Le Carpentier House. *See* Beauregard-Keyes House
Le Petit Salon 24, 47, 48
Le Petit Theatre du Vieux Carre 25, 48
Leveau, Marie 7
Lewis, Sinclair 25, 48, 70
Liveright, Horace 53
Loos, Anita 62
Loyola University 16

M

Madame John's Legacy 10, 27
Maison de Ville 46
Maple Street Book Store 17
Mardi Gras 7, 59, 69, 71
Martin, Mary 14
Maugham, W. Somerset 23, 59
Mayfair, Julian 9
Maylie, Anna May 71
Meat Market 62
Millay, Edna St. Vincent 23, 59
Miller, Cincinnatus. *See* Joaquin Miller
Miller, Joaquin 12, 14
Monteleone Hotel 35

Moon Walk 55
Moore, Lorrain Welein 49

N

Napoleon House 24, 33
New Orleans Aquarium 55
New Orleans Picayune 35, 48
Nicholson, Elizabeth 35, 48
NOLA Express 32
Nolte, Vincent 40

O

O. Henry 52–53, 56–58, 64, 65, 72
Old Congo Square 25
Old U.S. Mint 30
O'Neill, Eugene 46
Outsider 32

P

Parker, Dorothy 70
Percy, Walker 14, 16, 17, 53, 54
Picasso, Pablo 14
Place de St. Charles 69–71
Pontalba Buildings 23
Pontchartrain Hotel 14
Pool and Patio Apartments 27–28
Porter, Katherine Anne 23

Porter, William Sidney. *See* O. Henry
Priestly, J. B. 24

R

Ransom, John Crowe 59
Restaurant de la Tour Eiffel 14
Rice, Anne 9, 14, 15, 17, 54
Rivers, Pearl 72. *See* Elizabeth Nicholson
Roosevelt Hotel 71
Rouquette, Adrien 36–37, 51
Rouquette, Dominique 36–37

S

Saxon, Lyle 14, 25, 37–40, 44, 70–71, 72
Serling, Rod 14
'Sieur George's House 10, 42
Spratling, William 13, 14, 38, 60
St. Charles Hotel. *See* Place de St. Charles
St. Elizabeth's Home 15
St. Louis Cathedral 64
St. Louis Cemetery No. 1 53–54
St. Louis Hotel 41–42
Steinbeck, John 27
Stockton, Frank 36

Stone, Robert 17
Storyville 47
Stowe, Harriet Beecher 41
Stribling, T. S. 39
Stuart, Ruth McEnery 36
Styron, William 17

T

Tallant, Robert 27, 70
Tarkington, Booth 23, 59
Tate, Allen 59
Thackery, William Makepeace 69
Times-Democrat 50–51
Times-Picayune 37, 38–39, 44–45, 61, 70, 72
'Tite Poulette's Dwelling 10, 27
Toole, John Kennedy 16
Tulane University 16
Twain, Mark 9, 11–12, 14, 33, 41, 53, 64, 65

U

U.S. Custom House 33

V

Van Doren, Carl 17

W

Warner, Charles Dudley 11, 14
Warren, Robert Penn 59
Washington Artillery Park 55
Webb, Jon Edgar 32
Whitman, Jeff 67
Whitman, Walt 7, 41, 64, 67–70
Wilder, Thornton 49, 59
Williams, Tennessee 7, 14, 18, 19, 22, 24, 27–28, 30, 31, 33, 35, 37, 40, 42, 45–46, 48–49, 53, 58, 64, 71
Wilson, Edmund 59
Wolfe, Thomas 17, 71

Y

Young, Stark 39